THEATRE ARTS 1

Teacher's Course Guide

SECOND EDITION

ALAN ENGELSMAN
AND
PENNY ENGELSMAN

MERIWETHER PUBLISHING LTD.
Colorado Springs, Colorado

Meriwether Publishing Ltd., Publisher
P.O. Box 7710
Colorado Springs, CO 80933

Editorial coordinator: Rebecca Wendling
Typesetting: Sharon E. Garlock
Cover and book design: Tom Myers

ISBN 1-56608-032-0

© Copyright MCMXCVII Alpen and Jeffries Publishers
Printed in the United States of America
Second Edition

97 98 99   1 2 3 4 5

We dedicate this new *Theatre Arts 1 Teacher's Course Guide* to all theatre educators. You provide future actors with the tools of their trade: skills, ethics, and the opportunities to practice and hone their talents. You are hardworking, caring, devoted individuals. We recognize your labors. We recognize your commitment to theatre and education. We salute you!

In addition, we dedicate this textbook to Susan M. Enari of Anchorage, Alaska. She provided constant encouragement, concern, and love during the lengthy process of writing this new textbook. Susie offered support, common sense, humor, and hope! We thank Susie for her kindness and intelligence.

Contents

ACKNOWLEDGMENTS

Four poems by David Greenberg, "School Lunch," "Ape," "Hutton Mutton Glutton," and "A Couple of Things I Know." Used by permission of the author.

Poem, "Dog Days" by Grace Glicken. Used by permission of the author.

Poem, "Balloons Lifted High" by Robert L. Skrainka. Used by permission of the author.

Fable, "The Owl Who Was God" by James Thurber. Used by permission of Rosemary A. Thurber.

Adaptation from "The Bear" by Anton Chekov. Used by permission of the adapter, James Hoetker.

Rap, "Hey! I Can't Do That!" by Ginny Weiss. Used by permission of the author.

Grateful acknowledgment to Viola Spolin, whose pioneering work, *Improvisation for the Theatre*, has influenced countless teachers of drama.

UNIT ONE
Improvisation and Theatre Games

"Which activity will grab the students' attention when they first return to school from summer vacation?" "Which skills should a theatre teacher stress at the beginning of any semester?" "What will I teach this Monday?" These are just a few of the questions that many teachers ask themselves.

The *Theatre Arts 1* texts use improvisational exercises to introduce theatre education to high school and middle school students. Improvisational theatre exercises are just one method of initiating students into theatre education. Like other aspects of the theatre education curriculum, improvisational activities provide opportunities for students to learn thinking, listening, imagining, collaborating, and movement skills.

Each semester when you are teaching the improvisational section, some students may say, "These games are fun. But what do they have to do with theatre? What does this have to do with acting?" The *Theatre Arts 1 Student Handbook* and *Theatre Arts 1 Teacher's Course Guide* will answer these students' questions.

On the following page are two weekly calendars summarizing each day's activities. The calendar format is provided so that you can quickly review each week ahead of time or give a copy of your weekly syllabus to your principal or department chairperson if necessary.

Many theatre teachers are familiar with improvisation and theatre games. Some instructors recall when they themselves participated in improvisational exercises as students in a theatre course or workshop. However, other teachers have not had the opportunity to take a class or workshop which focuses on theatre games. These instructors may need an organized, structured semester syllabus.

Other instructors may be faced with teaching a course for which they are not fully trained. Some teachers may be newly assigned to the field of theatre education. Perhaps the teacher is an English teacher, a music instructor, or an art teacher.

Each semester when you are teaching the improvisational section, some students may say, "These games are fun. But what do they have to do with theatre? What does this have to do with acting?"

UNIT ONE: IMPROVISATION AND THEATRE GAMES

MONDAY	TUESDAY	WEDNESDAY	THURSDAY	FRIDAY
DAY ONE *WORKSHOP ONE* *ACTIVITIES #1 AND #2* (1) Briefly explain Workshop One objectives. Stress that students will enjoy the process of learning. (2) Complete Activity #1. Play "Traditional Tag" and variations. (3) Make Teacher Comments. (4) Begin Activity #2. Play "First Names Plus Flattering Adjective." *Reminder: Always bring your book to class.*	*DAY TWO* *WORKSHOP ONE* *ACTIVITIES #2 AND #3* (1) Ask students whether they know everyone's first name plus the flattering adjective? Allow several students to review class members' names and corresponding adjectives. (2) Continue Activity #2. Play "First and Last Names Plus Contact." (3) Begin Activity #3. Play "Czechoslovakia." Repeat chant using various accents.	*DAY THREE* *WORKSHOP ONE* *ACTIVITY #3* (1) Replay "Czechoslovakia." Repeat chant with various accents and focus on personas. (2) Continue Activity #3. Play Spolin's "Who Started the Motion?" (3) Next, play "Trust Fall." Game is described in detail in the *Student Handbook*. (4) Lastly, play Spolin's "Mirror Exercises." (5) If time, begin Workshop Two. Post objectives for Workshop Two on the board.	*DAY FOUR* *WORKSHOP TWO* *ACTIVITY #1* (1) Briefly review objectives for Workshop Two written on the board. (2) Begin Activity #1. Lead students in Spolin's "Play Ball." (3) Play Spolin's "Dodge Ball." (4) Continue with Spolin's "Three Changes." (5) Conclude with Spolin's "Mirror Exercise."	*DAY FIVE* *WORKSHOP TWO* *ACTIVITY #1* (1) Continue Activity #1. Divide students into pairs. (2) Review objectives and rules for "Blind Walk." (3) Allow students a short time to establish some nonverbal signals. (4) Send them on their "walk." (5) When all have returned, discuss experiences and discoveries. *Reminder: No talking.*

WEEK AT A GLANCE: WEEK ONE

UNIT ONE: IMPROVISATION AND THEATRE GAMES

MONDAY	TUESDAY	WEDNESDAY	THURSDAY	FRIDAY
DAY SIX *WORKSHOP THREE* *ACTIVITIES #1 AND #2* (1) Review objectives for Workshop Two. Have we met them? (2) Display Workshop Three objectives. (3) Complete Activity #1. Explain rules for "Where Game: Team Competition." (4) Divide class into two teams. Play "Where Game" (List A only). (5) Begin Activity #2. Play "Eating a Meal." Activity is described in the *Student Handbook*. Read aloud Activity #2's purpose from this *Teacher's Guide*.	*DAY SEVEN* *WORKSHOP THREE* *ACTIVITY #2* (1) As a warm-up, repeat "Where Game: Team Competition" (List B). (2) Continue Activity #2. Divide students into groups of five or six. Play "Word Charades." Follow the procedure outlined in your *Teacher's Guide* lesson plan. Use card sets A and B.	*DAY EIGHT* *WORKSHOP THREE* *ACTIVITY #3* (1) Begin Activity #3. Read aloud Activity #3's purpose from the *Teacher's Guide*. (2) Next, from the lesson plan, read aloud the objectives of "Difficulty With Small Objects." Play this game. (3) Explain the objectives of Spolin's "How Old Am I?" Choose four students to demonstrate activity. (4) Repeat Spolin's "How Old Am I?" with new players.	*DAY NINE* *WORKSHOP THREE* *ACTIVITY #3* (1) Repeat two favorite warm-ups. (2) Continue Activity #3. Choose other students to play Spolin's "How Old Am I?" Repeat activity until all students have participated. (3) Choose four students to demonstrate Spolin's "What Do I Do for a Living?" (4) Repeat Spolin's "What Do I Do for a Living?" using new players.	*DAY TEN* *WORKSHOP THREE* *ACTIVITY #3* (1) Use this day to complete Activity #3. You may wish to repeat "Word Charades" using lists C and D. (2) Review Workshop Three objectives. Have we met the objectives? (3) Have students read aloud the Unit One summary in the *Student Handbook*. Read aloud the eight skills learned. Students benefit from reviewing the skills they have learned.

WEEK AT A GLANCE: WEEK TWO

Improvisational games may be a new concept to them. The *Teacher's Guide* helps instructors teach their classes. It provides preparation ideas for each lesson, detailed lesson plans, and a thorough explanation of each activity's procedure. In addition, this syllabus offers instructors weekly calendars, commentary, and numerous in-class activities.

Instructors may be faced with teaching a course for which they are not fully trained.

NOTE

The *Theatre Arts 1 Teacher's Course Guide* and *Theatre Arts 1 Student Handbook* were written for both seasoned theatre educators and less experienced teachers of drama. Some instructors have had a great deal of experience teaching all aspects of theatre. This syllabus offers them fresh ideas and alternatives as well as a neatly constructed course plan, should they wish to utilize it. Even veteran teachers enjoy having someone else create their daily lesson plans or activities.

The newly assigned teacher no longer has to worry about gathering material and information to create each day's lesson plan. The *Teacher's Guide* provides everything the instructor needs to get started. Teachers can use this syllabus and the *Student Handbook* just as they are written. In the future, when they gain experience and confidence, instructors may wish to augment these texts with other materials or simply use the books as reference materials.

When discussing improvisation in the theatre classroom, this guide to teachers would be remiss if it did not mention a source book titled *Improvisation for the Theatre* written by Viola Spolin. Miss Spolin was truly a pioneer in theatre education. Instructors familiar with *Improvisation for the Theatre* often are able to recall Spolin games without having to consult her book. Other theatre teachers prefer to use more recent books as a guide to understanding and selecting theatre games. A variety of books on improvisational theatre games are available today.

However, some instructors have never heard the name Viola Spolin. They may feel uneasy about using improvisational games. These teachers are urged to examine a copy of Spolin's book at the library. Ask your school librarian to order the book for you. *Improvisation for the Theatre* summarizes Spolin's theatre games. Spolin and her students discovered that "theatre games" inspired both creativity and spontaneity.

Improvisation for the Theatre is a text that examines almost 200 games and activities. Spolin provides comments for most games. These observations explain how teachers can expect students to react to theatre games. Spolin has authored other texts. These books, however, contain much of the same information as her original text. Therefore, all references made to Viola Spolin's games in the *Theatre Arts 1 Teacher's Course Guide* will be references to *Improvisation for the Theatre* only. The *Teacher's Guide* will offer titles of certain games in Spolin's book. It will *not* provide descriptions of them.

> *Spolin and her students discovered that "theatre games" inspired both creativity and spontaneity.*

Helpful Teaching Tips

ONE Improvisation is an experimental activity. Experience enables all instructors to better understand which exercises work and which exercises do not seem to work as well. Understandably, instructors often create their own exercises to suit their needs.

TWO The *Theatre Arts 1* series has created its own theatre games. In past years the following seven games were printed on cards and sold separately: "The Where Game: Team Competition," "Word Charades," "Detailed Motives," "Adding Characters and Shifting Motives," "One Word Motives," "Christmas Rush," and "International Airport." The game cards for all seven original Engelsman Theatre Games are now reprinted *only* in the Appendix of this *Teacher's Guide*.

THREE The information contained on each game card is not included in the *Student Handbook*. Only the exercise objectives and the procedures appear in it.

FOUR Many other authors have since published fine books providing useful improvisational theatre exercises. View the following schedule of workshops as suggestions rather than prescriptions. Choose ideas from the many authors of improvisational theatre exercises. In that way you will determine which activities and procedures work best for the specific students you serve.

GROUND RULES FOR LEADERS OF IMPROVISATIONAL WORKSHOPS AND GAMES

Most class sessions need to begin with a warm-up activity. Several of the exercises listed in each workshop can serve as a warm-up. Ask a student who is an athlete, a dancer, or someone who practices yoga to share a warm-up that he or she has used in another setting. Warm-ups that prove to be popular and raise the group's energy level can and should be repeated in later lessons.

Skills improve when they are repeated. The leader should call the students' attention to skills that need repetition. Thus, repetition of skills at the beginning of each class session reinforces those skills and develops continuity.

Next, students thrive in an atmosphere of mutual trust and respect. Improvisational exercises work more smoothly when a teacher participates as an equal with the students. Optimum learning occurs when students perceive you as a willing participant as well as a leader.

Evaluations of exercises should come from the whole group. Words like "right" and "wrong" should be discouraged and avoided. Improvisations are experiments that sometimes succeed and sometimes fall flat. When they succeed, the entire group should acknowledge the fact and point to moments and feelings that seemed appropriate. When they fall flat, that, too, should be acknowledged. Nobody, however, should be singled out as having been the cause. The group may wish to try the exercise again or move on to a new one.

In all games a participant puts his/her energy into following rules, focusing on the point of concentration, and making the outcome a success. If the game works, there is an immediate sense of exhilaration. However, theatre games and athletic games differ when it comes to "non-successful" games. If the theatre game does not work, there are no long-term consequences. It merely was "not successful." The theatre players ought not view the outcome as a "failure."

If a student feels uncomfortable about joining a particular exercise, he or she should be allowed to sit out. Later you may wish to find out why the individual chose not to participate. Most of the exercises in the first four workshops involve the whole class working simultaneously. Therefore, individuals should not feel as if they are alone on stage. Nor should they

Ask a student who is an athlete, a dancer, or someone who practices yoga to share a warm-up that he or she has used in another setting.

All class members have a distinct job: to provide encouragement and support to every member of the class — especially the more timid members.

feel as if their talent or creativity is being judged. All class members have a distinct job: to provide encouragement and support to every member of the class — especially the more timid members.

Encourage students to dress casually so they can move freely or sit on the floor.

Stress safety! No rough contact. No intentional tricks. No one gets hurt.

WORKSHOP ONE: INTRODUCTORY GAMES

Objectives:	(1) Participants learn each others' names.
	(2) Participants lose inhibitions.
	(3) Participants develop group cohesion and trust.
	(4) Participants enjoy the process of learning through improvisational exercises.
Duration:	2 to 4 days
Improvisational Exercises:	
	Traditional Tag
	First Names Plus Flattering Adjective
	First and Last Names Plus Contact
	Czechoslovakia
	Trust Fall
Suggested Spolin games:	*Who Started the Motion*
	Mirror Exercise

ONE The chapters on improvisation have been divided into seven workshops which correspond to activities in the *Student Handbook*. Focusing on two to five learning objectives, each workshop continues for several class periods. A commentary on the selections and applications of activities accompanies each workshop outline.

TWO For hundreds of years, all over the world, children have been playing the game tag. They play tag in the streets, on school grounds, in courtyards, and on farms. Moreover, children creatively develop new versions of tag after a few short sessions.

THREE Children's street and playground games are excellent warm-up activities. Many improvisational exercises are based on such games. Encourage your students to find their own alternative warm-up activities.

Children's street and playground games are excellent warm-up activities.

ACTIVITY #1

Traditional Tag

Purpose:

Actors learn the importance of warming up, as athletes do.

Execution:

ONE At the beginning of Workshop One explain briefly the learning objectives for this workshop's activities. Stress the last objective: students will enjoy the process of learning through improvisational exercises. Inform your students that once they begin the exercises in Workshop One, there will be limited discussion of the learning objectives. At the close of Workshop One, review with the students the skills that they learned.

TWO *TRADITIONAL TAG:* Theatre teachers can use any game of tag as a good warm-up exercise. First establish playing area boundaries. Next, explain the rules:

- The last person to say "Not it" is "It."

- There are no "tag backs."

- Tell students the three safety rules: a) no rough contact; b) no intentional tricks; c) no one gets hurt.

THREE *TEACHER COMMENTS:* After three to five minutes of "play," state the following:

- This has been a warm-up exercise.

- Games are usually played just for fun. Theatre games are fun, but we can and do learn skills from these games.

- Improvisations are a type of game.

- From now on, there will be few, if any, explanations about what you are supposed to be learning. Merely concentrate on each game and its rules. Learning will occur.

We will discuss what we have learned from the games at the end of this chapter.

ACTIVITY #2

Learning & Remembering Classmates' Names

Purpose:

Actors learn names while losing inhibitions.

Execution:

ONE None of the learning objectives for Workshop One are written on the board. The purpose of Workshop One is to acclimate students to improvisational exercises. These two games may take the remainder of the class period. Students will be able to recall each other's name at the beginning of the next class session.

TWO *FIRST NAMES PLUS FLATTERING ADJECTIVE:* This game is described in detail in the *Student Handbook*. The text contains a complete explanation of the objectives and the procedure. The game reinforces one of the learning objectives stated for Workshop One. Participants will learn each others' first names.

THREE *FIRST AND LAST NAMES PLUS CONTACT:* This game is described in detail in the *Student Handbook*. The text contains a complete explanation of the objectives and the procedure. The game reinforces two of the learning objectives stated for Workshop One. Students will learn each other's names. Students will lose their inhibitions about participating in group activities.

Students will lose their inhibitions about participating in group activities.

ACTIVITY #3

Losing Inhibitions Through Movement

Purpose:

Actors lose inhibitions and develop group cohesion.

Execution:

ONE *CZECHOSLOVAKIA:* This rhythm game is an excellent warm-up exercise. The procedure and game are described in detail in the *Student Handbook*. An action exercise,

"Czechoslovakia" reinforces two learning objectives from Workshop One. Participants lose their inhibitions. Participants develop group cohesion. This activity may be introduced at the end of the first class session if time allows. If not, begin the second class period with "Czechoslovakia."

Participants develop concentration skills. Participants develop group cohesion.

TWO *WHO STARTED THE MOTION?:* This Spolin exercise reinforces two learning objectives from Workshop One. Participants develop concentration skills. Participants develop group cohesion. Try using this activity as a warm-up exercise. Both this game and "Czechoslovakia" may be used throughout this unit at the beginning of class sessions. Students become more skilled in "Who Started the Motion" each time it is repeated.

THREE *TRUST FALL:* The detailed procedure and game are described in the *Student Handbook.* "Trust Fall" reinforces two learning objectives from Workshop One. Participants lose their inhibitions. Participants develop group cohesion.

FOUR This version of "Trust Fall" is only one of many variations of the game. The following individuals will be able to describe several alternative procedures: your students, a physical education teacher, a scout leader, or someone in charge of outdoor education.

FIVE *MIRROR EXERCISES:* Viola Spolin describes many mirror exercises in *Improvisation for the Theatre.* The mirror exercises reinforce one learning objective from Workshop One. Participants begin to lose their inhibitions. Spolin's mirror games and variations are important to repeat and refine throughout Unit One. The exercises are fine warm-up

The publisher acknowledges the political changes that have occurred and recognizes the fact that neither Czechoslovakia nor Yugoslavia presently exist. The publisher still advises using these names or a substitute for the above game.

WORKSHOP TWO: SENSORY AWARENESS

Objectives: (1) Participants develop sensory awareness.

(2) Participants develop concentration skills.

(3) Participants continue to lose inhibitions and develop group cohesion.

Duration: 2 to 3 days

Improvisational Exercises:

Blind Walk

Suggested Spolin games: *Play Ball; Dodge Ball; Three Changes; Mirror Exercises*

Before the first sessions of Workshop Two, post the three workshop objectives on the blackboard or bulletin board. These objectives remain on display until the beginning of Workshop Three.

ACTIVITY #1

Using Games to Enhance Sense Memory

Purpose:

Actors learn to concentrate and to awaken their senses.

Execution:

Participants develop sensory awareness.

ONE *THREE SPOLIN GAMES: PLAY BALL; DODGE BALL; THREE CHANGES:* These Spolin exercises reinforce the following Workshop Two learning objectives. Participants develop sensory awareness. Participants develop concentration skills. Participants focus on group cohesion. Try these three games as a warm-up sequence for the opening session of Workshop Two. You may wish to repeat them at a later session.

TWO *MIRROR EXERCISES:* Spolin's "Mirror Exercises" reinforce the following Workshop Two learning objectives. Participants develop sensory awareness. Participants develop concentration skills. The original mirror game and the variations are important to repeat and refine throughout the entire unit. They function well as warm-up activities. You may want to play slow, ballad-type music in the background as a pace- and mood-setting motivator.

THREE *BLIND WALK:* This exercise is described in detail in the *Student Handbook*. The exercise and follow-up discussion will take a full class period. "Blind Walk" reinforces the following Workshop Two learning objectives. Participants reawaken their senses. Participants develop concentration skills. Participants develop close group cohesion while losing their inhibitions. It is recommended that you introduce this activity after the warm-up exercises on Day Two of Workshop Two.

FOUR Questions to ask students at the conclusion of "Blind Walk":

- As the sighted partner, did you notice anything new that you had not observed or heard before this activity?

- As a guide to your "blind" partner, what did you observe about your environment?

- How responsible did you feel for your "blind" partner?

- Did you succeed in remaining totally silent?

- Did you succeed in keeping your eyes closed when you were the "blind" partner?

WORKSHOP THREE: PANTOMIME

Objectives: (1) Participants establish objects, places and people *without* the use of speech or concrete objects.

(2) Participants use their bodies and faces to communicate meaning and feelings without using spoken language.

Duration: 3 to 4 days

Improvisational Exercises:

The Where Game: Team Competition

Eating a Meal

Word Charades

Suggested Spolin games: *Difficulty With Small Objects; How Old Am I? What Do I Do for a Living?*

Participants establish objects, places and people without the use of speech or concrete objects.

The Where Game: Team Competition

Purpose:

Actors learn to establish objects, places, and people without speech or actual objects.

Preparation:

ONE   Before the first sessions of Workshop Three, post the two workshop objectives on the blackboard or bulletin board. These objectives remain on display until the beginning of Workshop Four.

> **"The Where Game: Team Competition" is one of the seven original Engelsman Theatre Games.**

TWO   *THE WHERE GAME: TEAM COMPETITION* is one of the seven original Engelsman Theatre Games. The game cards for all seven games are now reprinted only in the Appendix of this *Teacher's Guide*. In addition, the seven Engelsman Theatre Games are thoroughly explained in the related lesson plans in this text.

THREE   The *Theatre Arts 1 Student Handbook* does not include any of the Engelsman Theatre Game Cards. Only the exercise objective and the procedure appear in the *Student Handbook*.

FOUR   In the Appendix of this text, you will locate two sets of cards for the "The Where Game: Team Competition." For your convenience and to comply with copyright law, the pages are perforated at the spine of this book. After removing the game card pages, cut the cards along the dotted line.

FIVE   Use Stack A and Stack B for separate rounds of this game. Stack A may be played on one day. Stack B can be saved for another day.

SIX   The lists of "wheres" have been carefully crafted for your class. The early cards are easier than the later cards. The team participants can expect the "wheres" to become more abstract and difficult as they progress through the cards.

Execution:

ONE *THE WHERE GAME: TEAM COMPETITION:* This game is one of the seven original Engelsman Theatre Games. Game cards for "The Where Game: Team Competition" appear in the Appendix of this book.

TWO The *Theatre Arts 1 Student Handbook* does *not* include any of the Engelsman Theatre Game Cards. The student text prints only the exercise objectives and the procedure for "The Where Game: Team Competition."

THREE "The Where Game: Team Competition" reinforces the following Workshop Three learning objective. Participants establish objects and places without the use of speech or concrete objects. This is a high energy game that moves rapidly. Use "The Where Game: Team Competition" as a warm-up exercise at the beginning of class.

FOUR Divide the class into two teams. Each team is located at different ends of the room. "The Where Game: Team Competition" is similar to charades. One participant from each team comes to the center of the room.

FIVE The instructor holds Stack A of the 3" x 5" cards that he/she created prior to this activity. Next, the instructor shows each team's volunteer the same "where" phrase. Example: in a rowboat.

SIX The first volunteers return to their teams. Without speech, each volunteer demonstrates the same phrase for his/her team. The first team to guess the "where" earns a point.

SEVEN The process is repeated with new volunteers until everyone on the team has played. You will keep score for both teams.

EIGHT Though they have been forewarned in their text, the actors have to be reminded through side-coaching about remaining *inside* an object. The *Student Handbook* indicates that the instructor will subtract two points from a team's score if the pantomimist establishes a "where" from the *outside* rather than the inside of an object.

For example, let's say a player places clothes into an imaginary washing machine. You subtract two points for "inside a washing machine." The actor must establish the idea of his body being inside a washing machine!

Participants establish objects and places without the use of speech or concrete objects. This is a high energy game that moves rapidly.

ACTIVITY #2

Eating a Meal and Word Charades

Purpose:

Actors learn to establish objects, places, and people without speech or actual items.

Preparation:

"Word Charades" is one of the seven original Engelsman Theatre Games.

ONE "Word Charades" is one of the seven original Engelsman Theatre Games. All of the cards for this game are reprinted in the Appendix of this book. In addition, this text provides a thorough explanation of the "Word Charades" game in the following lesson plan.

TWO The *Theatre Arts 1 Student Handbook* does not include any of the Engelsman Theatre Game Cards. Only the exercise objectives and the procedure appear in the *Student Handbook*.

THREE For your convenience and to comply with copyright law, the Appendix Englesman Game Card pages are perforated at the spine of this book. Remove the game card pages. Then cut the cards along the dotted line.

Execution:

ONE *EATING A MEAL:* This exercise is described in detail in the *Student Handbook*. The text contains a complete explanation of the objectives and the procedure. One variation of this game is also included in the *Theatre Arts 1 Student Handbook*. "Eating a Meal" reinforces and focuses on the following Workshop Three learning objective. Participants establish objects without the use of speech or concrete objects.

TWO *WORD CHARADES:* This game is one of the seven original Engelsman Theatre Games. The twenty-four game cards for the "Word Charades" cards appear only in the Appendix of this book.

The game cards are not included in the student text. Only the exercise objectives and the procedure appear in the *Student Handbook*.

THREE "Word Charades" reinforces the following Workshop Three learning objective. Participants establish objects and places without the use of speech or concrete objects. This is a high-energy game that moves rapidly. Use "Word Charades" as a warm-up exercise at the beginning of class. This exercise and discussion will take a full class period.

FOUR Divide the class into teams of five or six members. Two teams will compete while others observe. Therefore, Teams C and D will observe while Teams A and B are competing.

FIVE Team A should be sent out of the room so Team A cannot see or hear Team B in action. Team A does *not* return to the room until Team B has completed four words. Teams C and D remain in the audience observing.

SIX Team B: Three members are actors and two or three members are guessers. The guessers are seated side by side. They may talk and ask questions of the actors.

SEVEN From behind the guessers the instructor will hold up a card from Set A. This card will display the word (or compound word) to be acted out. *Rule for the Game*: Only one actor pantomimes an action at any time. The guessers will shout out the word or a synonym or a part of the word. When students guess the word, the instructor will hold up a second word. Another actor should begin the new pantomime.

EIGHT This process continues until four words have been guessed or three minutes have elapsed (whichever occurs first). Call Team A into the room. Using the same procedure, Team A tries to guess the same four words. The team that guesses all four words in the least amount of time is the winner of the competition.

NINE Repeat the competition with Teams C and D. Use Set B with these teams. Save Sets C, D, E, and F for later competitions.

TEN Instructors may wish to use a stopwatch when playing this game. At times an actor may be unable to communicate the meaning of the word that the instructor displays. If that happens, a second actor can replace the first actor. Or a third actor can replace the second one. In either case, the new actor can try a different approach. However, participants must remember the *Rule for the Game:* only one actor can perform at a time. If two performers pantomime the word at the same time, a fifteen-second penalty is imposed.

Participants establish objects and places without the use of speech or concrete objects.

More Pantomime Activities

Purpose:

Actors learn to establish objects and to express meaning through pantomime.

Execution:

ONE *DIFFICULTY WITH SMALL OBJECTS:* This Spolin exercise focuses on the following learning objective for Workshop Three. Participants establish objects through pantomime. The game should be repeated several times with different students participating. Good side-coaching can help players focus on the point of concentration.

> **Good side-coaching can help players focus on the point of concentration.**

TWO *TWO SPOLIN GAMES: HOW OLD AM I? WHAT DO I DO FOR A LIVING?* These Spolin exercises focus on the following learning objectives for Workshop Three. Students establish a "who" through pantomime. Participants use their bodies and faces as tools to communicate meanings and feelings without using spoken language. These games should be repeated several times with different students participating. When playing "How Old Am I?", it may be preferable to have participants pick an age out of a hat rather than giving them a choice of the age they will portray. Good side-coaching can help players focus on the point of concentration.

NOTE

Seasoned theatre teachers know that there is no one definitive, sure-fire activity that will motivate all students every time. Moreover, there is nothing written in stone that says you must begin a theatre course with improvisation. In fact, you may wish to open your curriculum with playwriting one year, storytelling the second year, and puppetry the third year.

You can jump-start your theatre course with many proven, motivating, educational activities. Theatre curriculum lends itself to diversity, variation, and creativity. These are the very characteristics that make theatre education a changing, growing, and challenging arena of learning.

Theatre curriculum lends itself to diversity, variation, and creativity.

UNIT SUMMARY

Unit One introduced students to improvisational theatre activities. Actors learned to interact with other performers. Participants also learned to communicate in pantomime. The three improvisational workshops you completed were titled: *Introductory Games, Sensory Awareness,* and *Pantomime.*

Following is a list of eight skills participants learned in this unit:

1. Learned each others' names.

2. Lost inhibitions.

3. Developed group cohesion and trust.

4. Enjoyed the process of learning through improvisational exercises.

5. Developed sensory awareness.

6. Developed concentration skills.

7. Established objects, places and people without the use of speech or concrete objects.

8. Used their bodies and faces to communicate meaning and feelings.

More Improvisation and Theatre Games

Unit Two presents four new workshops: Sound and Motion, Integrating Who, Where and What, Spontaneity, and More Complex Improvisations. Each workshop focuses on several learning objectives. Students develop essential skills as they participate in each exercise.

Unit Two examines and refines both new and previously learned skills. In Workshops Four, Five, Six and Seven students concentrate on twelve skills. Some of these competencies are integrating information with movement to enhance communications, exploring nonverbal aspects of speech that add meaning to language, developing scenes containing dramatic conflict, and developing a sense of ensemble acting.

Four weekly calendars summarizing each day's activities follow. The calendar format is provided for your convenience so that you can quickly review each week's activities ahead of time or give a copy of your weekly syllabus to your principal or department chairperson.

Unit Two presents four new workshops: Sound and Motion, Integrating Who, Where and What, Spontaneity, and More Complex Improvisations.

UNIT TWO: MORE IMPROVISATION AND THEATRE GAMES

MONDAY	TUESDAY	WEDNESDAY	THURSDAY	FRIDAY
DAY ONE *WORKSHOP FOUR ACTIVITIES #1 AND #2*	**DAY TWO** *WORKSHOP FOUR ACTIVITIES #2 , #3 AND #4*	**DAY THREE** *WORKSHOP FOUR ACTIVITIES #5 AND #6*	**DAY FOUR** *WORKSHOP FOUR ACTIVITY #6*	**DAY FIVE** *WORKSHOP FIVE ACTIVITY #1*
(1) Display objectives for Workshop Four. (2) Begin Activity #1. Play "Zeke-Zork." Steps one through five are in the *Student Handbook*. (3) Next, play the variation of "Zeke-Zork" described only in your *Teacher's Guide*. (4) Begin Activity #2. Play "Sound and Motion Emblems." (5) Continue Activity #2. Play "Sound and Motion Warm-ups."	(1) Briefly replay "Sound and Motion Emblems." (2) Next, replay "Sound and Motion Warm-ups." (3) Begin Activity #3. Introduce "Sound and Motion Sequence" described only in the *Teacher's Guide*. Demonstrate an appropriate crossover. (4) Play "Sound and Motion Sequence." Allow energy to build. (5) Begin Activity #4. Play the variations of "Sound and Motion Sequence." Four variations are described in the *Teacher's Guide*.	(1) Repeat "Zeke-Zork" exercise as a warm-up. (2) Begin Activity #5, "Abstract Machines." It is described in detail in the *Student Handbook*. (3) Next, introduce Activity #6, "Spolin Games." Play "Mirror Exercise #3."	(1) Start class with a favorite warm-up exercise. (2) Next, continue Activity #6. Introduce Spolin's "Contrapuntal Argument." Ask two volunteers to demonstrate the game. (3) Divide entire class into pairs. Several pairs play game at the same time. (4) Review Workshop Four objectives written on board.	(1) Begin Workshop Five — Activity #1: Write the workshop objectives on board. (2) Next, class reads aloud the section "Developing Scenes Containing Dramatic Conflicts" located in the *Student Handbook*. (3) Follow procedure for Activity #1. (4) Demonstrate Spolin's "Where Through Three Objects." One actor at a time establishes a "where."

WEEK AT A GLANCE: WEEK THREE

© Alpen & Jeffries 1997

UNIT TWO: MORE IMPROVISATION AND THEATRE GAMES

MONDAY	TUESDAY	WEDNESDAY	THURSDAY	FRIDAY
DAY SIX *WORKSHOP FIVE ACTIVITY #1*	**DAY SEVEN** *WORKSHOP FIVE ACTIVITY #2*	**DAY EIGHT** *WORKSHOP FIVE ACTIVITY #2*	**DAY NINE** *WORKSHOP FIVE ACTIVITY #3*	**DAY TEN** *WORKSHOP FIVE ACTIVITY #3*
(1) Display objectives for Workshop Five. (2) Warm up with "Czechoslovakia." (3) Continue Activity #1. (4) Play Spolin's "Add an Object: Where #1." (5) Divide class into two teams. Play "Add an Object: Where #2." (6) Next, ask two students to demonstrate Spolin's "Who" game. (7) Repeat with many pairs of students. (8) Discuss whether actors successfully created a "who" and "where"? Can you identify their motives?	(1) Begin Activity #2. Introduce "Detailed Motives." Students read aloud procedure described in the *Student Handbook*. (2) Two students demonstrate game by improvising a scene prompted by Cards 1A and 1B. Teacher offers side coaching. (3) Viewers discuss the characters' motives. (4) Divide class into three teams. Follow detailed instructions in the *Teacher's Guide*.	(1) Return to "Detailed Motives." Have students recreate successful scenes from yesterday. (2) Discuss what helped make the scenes a success. (3) Let new players create new scenes using new pairs of cards. (4) Groups gather to view new scenes. (5) Viewers discuss scenes using the words "who," "where" and "what."	(1) Begin Activity #3. Introduce "One-Word Motives" game. (2) Students read game objective and detailed procedure in the *Student Handbook*. (3) Two students demonstrate game. (4) Begin to play "One-Word Motives" game. Follow the detailed instructions in this *Teacher's Guide*. (5) Participants play game in pairs. Rest of class becomes the audience.	(1) You may want to continue Activity #3. (2) After a pair performs, ask if the characters' motives were clear? (3) Have other pairs create scenes based on "One Word-Motives" cards. (4) Review Workshop Five objectives. Have we created scenes with conflict?

WEEK AT A GLANCE: WEEK FOUR

© Alpen & Jeffries 1997

UNIT TWO: MORE IMPROVISATION AND THEATRE GAMES

MONDAY	TUESDAY	WEDNESDAY	THURSDAY	FRIDAY
DAY ELEVEN *WORKSHOP SIX* *ACTIVITIES #1 AND #2*	*DAY TWELVE* *WORKSHOP SIX* *ACTIVITY #2*	*DAY THIRTEEN* *WORKSHOP SIX* *ACTIVITY #2*	*DAY FOURTEEN* *WORKSHOP SIX* *ACTIVITY #3*	*DAY FIFTEEN* *WORKSHOP SEVEN* *ACTIVITY #1 AND #2*
(1) Post Workshop Six objectives on board. (2) Begin Activity #1. Follow the Lesson Plan for Activity #1 in this *Teacher's Guide.* (3) Lead students in two warm-up exercises. (4) Next, have students read directions and procedure for "Adding Characters and Shifting Motives." (5) Announce actors in each of the four scenes.	(1) Lead students in two more warm-up exercises in Activity #1. (2) Next, begin Activity #2. Divide class into groups of six. Play Activity #2, "Adding Characters and Shifting Motives." (3) One group performs at a time. Other students become audience. (4) Follow Lesson Plan procedure in this *Teacher's Guide.* (5) Discuss successful moments in scenes.	(1) Lead students in two favorite warm-up exercises. (2) Continue Activity #2, "Adding Characters and Shifting Motives." (3) One group performs at a time. Other teams become the audience. (4) Follow Lesson Plan procedure for Activity #2 in this *Teacher's Guide.* (5) Discuss successful moments following each scene.	(1) Begin Activity #3. It does not involve game cards. (2) Follow the Activity #3 Lesson Plan in this *Teacher's Guide.* (3) Students read game objective and procedure in the *Student Handbook.* (4) Play "Transformations." (5) Next, repeat "One Word Motives." (6) Lastly, read the Workshop Six objectives aloud. Ask students if objectives were met.	(1) Write Workshop Seven learning objectives on the board. (2) Begin Activity #1. It is a preliminary exercise prior to "Christmas Rush." (3) Students participate in "Sound and Motion Give and Take" and Spolin's "Two Scenes" as a warm-up activity. (4) Next, begin Activity #2, "Christmas Rush." Distribute twelve cards to actors. (5) Follow Lesson Plan for Activity #2 in this *Teacher's Guide.* Ask the questions provided in the instructions.

WEEK AT A GLANCE: WEEK FIVE

UNIT TWO: MORE IMPROVISATION AND THEATRE GAMES

MONDAY	TUESDAY	WEDNESDAY	THURSDAY	FRIDAY
DAY SIXTEEN *WORKSHOP SEVEN* *ACTIVITY #3*	*DAY SEVENTEEN* *WORKSHOP SEVEN* *ACTIVITY #3*			
(1) Begin Activity #3, "International Airport." At random, distribute the fifteen character cards to actors. Appoint one or two Flight Information Attendants. (2) Distribute Fact Sheet to the fifteen characters only. They need to fill out the sheet completely. (3) Follow detailed instructions for Activity #3 in this *Teacher's Guide.* (4) If there is time, discuss scene at completion of activity.	(1) Continue with discussion of "International Airport." (2) Note questions in the *Teacher's Guide.* (3) Have students read aloud the Unit Summary for Unit Two in the *Student Handbook.* Read aloud all fifteen skills learned in Unit Two. Students benefit from reviewing the skills they have learned.			

WEEK AT A GLANCE: WEEK SIX

WORKSHOP FOUR: SOUND AND MOTION

Participants explore nonverbal aspects of speech (such as pitch, tone, and facial expression) to add meaning to language.

Objectives: (1) Participants strengthen memory and listening skills.

(2) Participants learn to respond rapidly to nonverbal symbols.

(3) Participants experience the range and power of vocal expression.

(4) Participants use movement to enhance communication.

(5) Participants explore nonverbal aspects of speech (such as pitch, tone, and facial expression) to add meaning to language.

Duration: 4 days

Improvisational Exercises:

Zeke-Zork

Sound and Motion Emblems

Sound and Motion Warm-Ups

Sound and Motion Sequence

Abstract Machines

Suggested Spolin games: *Mirror Exercise #3*
                         Contrapuntal Argument

Before the first session of Workshop Four, post the five workshop objectives on the blackboard or bulletin board. These objectives remain on display until the beginning of Workshop Five.

Prior to Activity #1, familiarize yourself with the game "Zeke-Zork" and its variations. The activity will work more smoothly if you understand the procedure.

Zeke-Zork Activity

Purpose:

Actors sharpen listening skills and respond spontaneously with appropriate verbal sounds and intonations.

Execution:

ONE *ZEKE-ZORK* is a warm-up activity and should be repeated on successive days. "Zeke-Zork" is described in detail in the *Student Handbook.* Present the directions orally rather than have the students read them in advance. This exercise and discussion may require a full class period.

> *Participants experiment with the range and power of vocal expression.*

TWO *ZEKE-ZORK* reinforces the following Workshop Four learning objectives: Participants experiment with the range and power of vocal expression. Participants explore nonverbal aspects of speech (such as pitch, tone, and facial expression) to add meaning to language.

THREE Variation for "Zeke-Zork": This variation is not included in the *Student Handbook.* The variation and explanation appear only in this *Teacher's Guide.* Remember there is a pattern change for the participants' positions.

FOUR Pattern Variation for "Zeke-Zork."

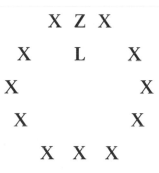

FIVE L represents the leader who is facing Z, one of the participants standing in a circle. L says "Zeke-Zork" to Z. Z must repeat "Zork" back to L. Then this person has the option of turning to her left or right or maintaining eye contact with the leader for the second part of the word "Zeke-Zork."

SIX If the leader is the recipient of the return message, he/she may either bounce the message back to Z or bounce the message to one of the participants to the left or right of Z.

Thus, each person receiving the "Zeke-Zork" message may pass it on to any one of three players.

SEVEN If students get tired of the "Zeke-Zork" sounds, try substituting "Ping-Pong" or "Glip-Glop."

ACTIVITY #2

Sound and Motion Games

Purpose:

Actors use motion to enhance communication, strengthen memory and listening skills, and explore nonverbal aspects of speech.

Execution:

ONE *SOUND AND MOTION EMBLEMS:* This is a transition game. It prepares students for the "Sound and Motion Warm-up." The *Student Handbook* has a detailed description of "Sound and Motion Emblems."

TWO "Sound and Motion Emblems" reinforces the following Workshop Four learning objectives:

- Participants strengthen memory and listening skills.

- Participants experiment with the range and power of vocal expression.

- Participants use motion to enhance communication.

- Participants explore nonverbal aspects of speech to augment communication.

- Participants learn to respond rapidly with nonverbal symbols.

Participants explore nonverbal aspects of speech to augment communication.

THREE *SOUND AND MOTION WARM-UP:* This exercise reinforces the following Workshop Four learning objectives:

- Participants strengthen memory and listening skills.

- Participants respond rapidly to nonverbal symbols.

- Participants experiment with the range and power of vocal expression.

- Participants use movement to enhance communication.

- Participants explore nonverbal aspects of speech (e.g.,

pitch, tone, and facial expressions) to add meaning to language.

FOUR Warm-up activities sharpen the bodies and the minds of the participants. A distinguishing feature of the "Sound and Motion Warm-Up" is that everyone is simultaneously involved in the sound and motion process.

FIVE Everyone must remain alert to the gradual changes that each new leader introduces. Like "Zeke-Zork," this warm-up can be repeated on successive days. Introduce this game as a warm-up anytime you wish to raise student energy levels and to exercise actors' vocal chords as well as their bodies.

> *Warm-up activities sharpen the bodies and the minds of the participants.*

ACTIVITY #3

Sound and Motion Sequence Theatre Game

Purpose:

Actors use motion to enhance communication, strengthen memory and listening skills, and explore nonverbal aspects of speech.

Preparation:

ONE *SOUND AND MOTION SEQUENCE:* This exercise is not included in the *Student Handbook.* The directions and the actual exercise appear only in this *Teacher's Guide.* Participants should not know where the exercise is leading. Prior to class, read the following directions. Familiarize yourself with the procedure for "Sound and Motion Sequence."

TWO "Sound and Motion Sequence" reinforces all five objectives in Workshop Four.

THREE "Sound and Motion Warm-up" was designed to be used as a preliminary activity to the "Sound and Motion Sequence" game. Therefore, as noted on your weekly planning calendar, schedule this activity on the same day as the "Sound and Motion Sequence." Play the warm-up directly before you begin "Sound and Motion Sequence."

FOUR Because of the energy and volume that builds during the session, conduct this exercise in an area where high voice levels will not disturb other classes. Students often become exuberant during this exercise.

Execution:

ONE "Sound and Motion Sequence" is not included in the *Student Handbook*. The directions and the actual exercise appear only in this *Teacher's Guide*. Participants should not know where the exercise is leading.

TWO "Sound and Motion Sequence" reinforces the following Workshop Four learning objectives:

- Participants strengthen memory and listening skills.

- Participants respond rapidly to nonverbal symbols.

- Participants experiment with the range and power of vocal expression.

- Participants use movement to enhance communication.

- Participants explore nonverbal aspects of speech (e.g., pitch, tone, and facial expressions) to add meaning to language.

THREE To begin this activity have the class form two equal lines facing each other across a neutral playing area ten to twelve feet in width.

FOUR Two or three volunteers and/or the instructor begin a sound and motion — like the ones used in the previous exercise. They carry the sound and motion across the neutral playing area to any one of the participants lined up on the other side. See the following diagram.

FIVE Diagram for "Sound and Motion Sequence"

X = participant   V = volunteer

X X V X X X X X X X X X

V X X X X X X X X X V X

If you have difficulty recruiting volunteers, begin the exercise with a sound and motion of your own.

SIX If you have difficulty recruiting volunteers, begin the exercise with a sound and motion of your own. After you pass it on to one participant in the opposite line, return with a new sound and motion to a second participant across the way. It is best to have three participants doing their distinct sound and motions at the same time.

SEVEN The volunteer stands in front of a participant on the opposing side. She continues with the sound and motion until the new player picks it up and moves out into the neutral playing area. The original volunteer then fills the vacant space in the line and becomes silent.

EIGHT As the new player crosses the neutral area, he/she allows the mirrored sound and motion to evolve into a slightly altered one. This evolution of sound and motion is much the same as participants experienced in the "Sound and Motion Warm-Up."

NINE This altered sound and motion is then carried across to any player in the opposite line. The process of transferal, exchanging places, and allowing the sound and motion to evolve into something new is repeated again and again. With three sound and motions being transferred all the time, it is not unusual for one player to be selected as a carrier several times. When chosen, the instructor should find someone across the way who has not been selected.

ACTIVITY #4

Sound and Motion Sequence Game

Purpose:

Actors use motion to enhance communication, strengthen memory and listening skills, and explore nonverbal aspects of speech.

Execution:

ONE These exercises are not included in the *Student Handbook*. The directions and the actual exercises appear only in this *Teacher's Guide*. Participants should not have foreknowledge of where the exercise is leading.

TWO Following are four variations for the "Sound and Motion Sequence" exercise. As noted previously, because of the energy and volume that evolves, conduct this exercise in an area where high voice levels will not disturb other classes. Students often become exuberant.

Actors use motion to enhance communications, strengthen memory and listening skills, and explore nonverbal aspects of speech.

THREE *Variation A*

"When I tell you to begin again, continue as you have before. However, this time, have your sound and motion reflect joy, anger, or suspicion."

After the players have learned and understood the basic pattern of transferal, exchanging places, cross over, evolving into a new sound and motion, and exchange, you shout, "Freeze!" Then introduce the following instruction: "When I tell you to begin again, continue as you have before. However, this time, have your sound and motion reflect joy, anger, or suspicion. Begin again."

FOUR *Variation B*

Allow Variation A to continue. Side coach to remind participants of the three emotions — joy, anger, and suspicion. Then, freeze the players. Tell them to continue expressing the emotions, with broad gestures or movement. However, in place of the nonverbal sounds, tell students to use the word *yes* or *no*. Begin again.

FIVE *Variation C*

After students experience and understand Variation B, explain Variation C. Now players in the waiting line, who have been approached by the participants crossing the neutral area, respond to the *yes* and *no* rather than imitate it. The players should carry that response all the way across the neutral area. On the other side, the waiting participants respond to the player. They then carry that response across. The instructor continues to coach participants to express joy, anger, or suspicion.

SIX *Variation D*

> As a final round, the words *yes* and *no* should be replaced by any short phrase. A player says the phrase in response to the words that the crossing player is shouting. (As players shout, they should be emphasizing their short phrases with strong body and limb movements.) Inhibitions may be reduced during this game phase.

SEVEN The discussion following the exercise needs to examine the manner in which sound and motion complement one another. In most acting situations performers will not shout all of their lines. On this day, however, students are encouraged to explore ways in which the body reinforces what the voice is expressing.

In most acting situations performers will not shout all of their lines.

ACTIVITY #5

Abstract Machines

Purpose:

Actors experiment with the range and power of vocal expression, use movement to enhance communication, and explore nonverbal aspects of speech.

Execution:

ONE The game "Abstract Machines," is described in detail in the *Student Handbook*.

TWO "Abstract Machines" reinforces the following Workshop Four learning objectives:

- Participants experiment with the range and power of vocal expression.

- Participants use movement to enhance communication.

- Participants explore nonverbal aspects of speech to augment communication.

THREE Activity #5 encourages students to share in the creation of an elaborate "machine" consisting of human moving parts and strange, albeit appropriate, sounds.

FOUR Divide the class into groups of seven or eight. One group performs at a time. The other students serve as an audience. Member A of the performing group moves Stage Center. She begins a simple repeated sound and motion. For example, she walks raising and lowering an arm and a leg while at the same time repeating the sound, "shlunk, shlunk, shlunk." This is the first moving part of an abstract machine.

FIVE Member B joins Member A on stage. Member B creates a motion that interacts with Member A's movements. Member B also adds a new sound. Member C then joins the action. He adds to the machine as a moving part. He may interact with either Member A or B, or both A and B. Member C must create an additional sound.

SIX Other members of the group add moving parts and sounds to the machine. Students should add motions and sounds one at a time. However, all members of a group must participate. The exercise should be completed within a minute or two. Then another group creates a new abstract machine.

> *Students should add motions and sounds one at a time.*

ACTIVITY #6
Spolin Games

Purpose:

Actors use movement to enhance communication, and explore nonverbal aspects of speech.

Execution:

ONE MIRROR EXERCISE #3: Spolin's "Mirror Exercise #3" is an extension of her other mirror games. Participants are able to explore nonverbal aspects of speech, particularly facial expression, to add meaning to language. "Mirror Exercise #3" enables students to sharpen their observation and listening skills.

TWO CONTRAPUNTAL ARGUMENT: This Spolin exercise reinforces the following Workshop Four learning objectives:

- Participants use movement to enhance communication.

- Participants explore nonverbal aspects of speech to augment communication. Initially, ask two volunteers to demonstrate "Contrapuntal Argument."

Then, in pairs, everybody can try the activity simultaneously. Conduct this activity in an area where high voice levels will not disturb other classes because students often become exuberant during this exercise.

WORKSHOP FIVE: INTEGRATING WHO, WHERE & WHAT

Objectives: (1) Participants reinforce the concepts of *where* and *who* in early scene work which incorporates both pantomime and speech.

(2) Participants develop scenes containing dramatic conflict.

(3) Participants introduce a *what*, a motive.

Duration: 6 days

Improvisational Exercises:

> ***Detailed Motives***
>
> ***One Word Motives***

Suggested Spolin games: *Where Through Three Objects*
Add an Object Where #1 and #2
Who Game

ONE Before the first session of Workshop Five, post the three workshop objectives on the blackboard or bulletin board. These objectives remain on display until the beginning of Workshop Six.

TWO You may notice that some students volunteer all the time. Others shyly hold back. Involve all students as much as possible. Students build on each other's strengths. Together they become a dynamic unit.

THREE Beginning with Workshop Five the improvisations begin to evolve into recognizable scene work. Workshop Five primarily concentrates on an integration of *who, where,* and *what*. However, it is important to remind students that scenes often begin with an actor establishing a *where* using pantomime.

> *You may notice that some students volunteer all the time. Others shyly hold back. Involve all students as much as possible. Students build on each other's strengths.*

ACTIVITY #1

Using Pantomime

Using pantomime, actors first reinforce the concepts of where and who and then introduce a what (a motive), into basic scene work.

Purpose:

Using pantomime, actors first reinforce the concepts of *where* and *who* and then introduce a *what* (a motive), into basic scene work.

Execution:

ONE Have students read out loud the pages in Unit Two of the *Student Handbook* titled "Developing Scenes Containing Dramatic Conflict." Students will have a better understanding of a concept if they read it aloud.

TWO Explain to the class that, when two or more people are on-stage and the rest of the class is watching, risk-taking is involved. Urge audience members to be supportive rather than critical. If a particular activity doesn't quite succeed, consider the effort a noble experiment. Then try it again.

THREE WHERE THROUGH THREE OBJECTS/ADD AN OBJECT WHERE #1 AND #2: These Spolin exercises reinforce the following learning objective stated for Workshop Five:

- Participants reinforce the concepts of *where* in basic scene work using pantomime. In her book, *Improvisation for the Theatre*, Spolin devotes a whole chapter to the importance of establishing a *where*. Have students demonstrate "Where Through Three Objects." The entire class plays. One actor at a time establishes a *where*.

FOUR WHO GAME: In this Spolin exercise participants introduce a *what*, a motive, into basic scene work using pantomime and speech. There are only two characters in this Spolin exercise. Repeat the exercise with many pairs of students. Use the "Who Game" as a preliminary activity to the next exercise "Detailed Motives." Have two students demonstrate the "Who Game." Repeat with many pairs of students.

ACTIVITY #2

Detailed Motives

Purpose:

Students learn to integrate *who, where,* and *what* in a scene.

Preparation:

ONE All forty individual character cards for "Detailed Motives" are reprinted in the Appendix of this book. In addition, this *Teacher's Guide* provides a thorough explanation of the "Detailed Motives" game.

TWO The *Student Handbook* does not include any of the Engelsman Theatre Game Cards. The *Student Handbook* prints only the exercise objectives and the procedure for this game.

THREE Prior to Activity #2, divide your class into groups of six. Mix experienced or confident actors with shy or reluctant actors. Try to create congenial diversity in each group. Students build on each other's strengths. Record the names of students in each group.

FOUR On the day of the activity, some instructors like to separate their groups into different rooms or areas. Other teachers like to keep the groups in one environment where they can see each group on task. Again, you choose the best method to meet your needs and the needs of your students and principal.

...You choose the best method to meet your needs and the needs of your students and principal.

FIVE Choose the location where you wish all four or five groups to meet at the completion of their improvisation sessions. The area can be as simple as the middle of the room. Planning details ahead of time helps students succeed in this activity.

SIX The "Detailed Motives" exercise reinforces the following Workshop Five learning objectives:

- Participants develop scenes containing dramatic conflict.

- Participants introduce a *what*, a motive.

SEVEN This activity provides ample opportunities for students to learn, to be creative, and to laugh. Prior to the day you introduce "Detailed Motives," familiarize yourself with the procedure for playing this game. Preplanning saves time and ensures the success of the exercise.

EIGHT Two actors will participate in each of the twenty different scenes. The first seven pairs of cards require one male and one female. On the remaining pairs of cards, the gender of each player is interchangeable.

NINE The forty character cards (twenty pairs) for "Detailed Motives" are reprinted in the Appendix of this text. The first seven pairs of cards require one male and one female. On the remaining pairs of cards, the gender of each player is interchangeable.

Execution:

ONE The "Detailed Motives" game reinforces the following Workshop Five learning objectives:

- Participants develop scenes containing dramatic conflict.

- Participants introduce a *what*, a motive.

TWO When you first introduce the game bring the forty "Detailed Motives" cards that you have removed from the back of this text. Each game consists of two cards. For example, cards are labeled 1A and 1B; 2A and 2B. Two actors will participate in each of the twenty different scenes.

THREE For each of the twenty scenes, the actor with the subscript A next to the number on his\her card begins the scene alone on-stage. Character A establishes the *where* of the scene. The procedure for establishing *where* is described in detail in the *Student Handbook*. Props should be pantomimed. However, on occasion, you may wish to provide an actual prop to help add to a performer's sense of realism and security. These props might include a necklace, a book, or a newspaper.

FOUR Randomly select two students. Choose one of the twenty situations. Give each actor a card.

You may want to side coach participants with the following comments:

- CURTAIN! Character A enters first. Focus on *who* you are and *where* you are. Help establish the *where* by pantomiming at least three objects in the room or area. Walk around the set. Establish furniture or objects in the *where*. Handle the furniture or objects as your

Props should be pantomimed. However, on occasion, you may wish to provide an actual prop to help add to a performer's sense of realism and security.

character would handle them.

• Character B, prepare to enter the scene. Consider in advance how you will establish and reinforce the *where*. Use at least one of the objects or pieces of furniture that Character A has established. You may wish to add another object to the scene.

• Character A and Character B, take a few moments to establish a relationship. Reinforce the *where*. Character A and Character B can and should speak to one another. Remember that your first priority is to establish *who* you are and *where* you are.

• Character A and Character B, slowly, gradually, let your *what*, your motive, develop in your minds. Think it, but do not announce your motive. Analyze your partner. In what way is she an obstacle to you? In what way is she an obstacle to your motive? Keep the scene alive. Keep your *what* alive. Show us. Do not tell us. Place your effort into achieving your motive. Character A and Character B, expect that your motives will bring you into some type of conflict. Thirty seconds until curtain. CURTAIN!

> **Keep the scene alive. Keep your what alive. Show us. Do not tell us.**

• End the scene after it seems to reach a climax. If the exercise appears to be stalling, bring it to a close. Either the performers or the instructor may call CURTAIN! to end the scene. Allow the actors to describe their understanding of their partner's motives. Call on the audience of class members to add their observations. Keep comments positive and supportive.

FIVE Now, divide the class into groups of six. Read the names of the students in each section. Each group has three pairs of actors.

SIX In each group, one pair performs at a time. The remaining four team participants become the audience for the actors. The individual cards tell the two actors *where* their scene takes place and *who* the two characters are. Each person, however, will read silently his or her motive, the *what*.

SEVEN Give each performer a card. The first seven pairs of cards require one male and one female. On the remaining cards, the gender of each player is interchangeable.

EIGHT The "Detailed Motives" situations contain varied motives designed to challenge a variety of students.

One Word Motives

Purpose:

Working unrehearsed, students learn to focus more fully on the *what* in each improvised situation.

Preparation:

ONE "One Word Motives": This activity is one of the seven original Engelsman Theatre Games. The cards for this game are printed in the Appendix of this *Teacher's Guide.* In addition, this book provides a thorough explanation of the "One Word Motives" game in the following lesson plan.

TWO The *Student Handbook* does not include any of the Engelsman Theatre Game Cards.

THREE Prior to Activity #3, divide your class into pairs. Record the names of students in each pair. As you have done before, try to mix experienced or confident actors with shy or reluctant actors.

FOUR Engelsman Game Card pages are perforated at the spine of this book. Remove the game card pages. Then cut the cards along the dotted line.

FIVE One person from each pair of performers will draw a card at random on the day this game is played. All other students become the audience.

> *One person from each pair of performers will draw a card at random on the day this game is played. All other students become the audience.*

Execution:

ONE The "One Word Motives" game reinforces the following Workshop Five learning objectives:

- Participants develop scenes containing dramatic conflict.

- Participants introduce a *what,* a motive.

TWO ONE WORD MOTIVES: Participants are divided into pairs. One pair performs at a time. All others become the audience.

THREE Character A leaves the room. Character B selects a card from the "One Word Motives" cards. The audience helps Character B choose a *where* and a *who* that are appropriate for her character and the motive she has chosen.

Character B also needs to determine the relationship between Character A and Character B in their scene. Therefore, Character B must determine the *who* that Character A is portraying.

FOUR Character A is called back into the room. Do not tell Character A about the decisions that Character B and the audience have made regarding Character A's behavior and character. The improvised scene begins with Character A on-stage.

FIVE Character B may request that Character A stand or sit as the scene begins. Character A remains neutral when Character B enters and begins talking. Character A uses phrases that are not specific when answering Character B's questions and comments.

SIX Character B avoids using words which directly identify the relationship between him/herself and Character A. For example, if he/she is the owner of a store and the employer of Character A, he/she should avoid referring to Character A as an employee. However, Character B could say, "Are you feeling better? We all missed you yesterday."

Character B also could say, "Several people have asked about you." These comments may begin to help Character A understand the relationship between Character A and Character B.

SEVEN Once Character B has established clues about the relationship with Character A, Character B pursues the "One Word Motive" on the drawn card. For example, if the motive is to learn the truth, Character B might say, "Yesterday, Tonia called to confirm your one o'clock luncheon date. She said she would just meet you at Pepe's."

EIGHT Once Character A is able to identify Character B's character, Character A might say, "She must have been confirming our date for next week." Next, Character A needs to determine his/her relationship to Character B. He/she needs to discover whether he/she is a customer or a relative or an employee of Character B. Once that is resolved, Character A needs to discover Character B's motive.

> *The audience helps Character B choose a where and a who that are appropriate for her character and the motive she has chosen.*

Both characters should seek to keep the scene stimulating.

NINE Both characters should seek to keep the scene stimulating. The instructor will call CURTAIN! to end scenes in which the motive becomes obscured. Players may also end their own scenes.

TEN If Character A misidentifies the relationship to Character B, Character B may take one of the following actions:

- Character B can end the scene.

- Character B could try to correct Character A's mistake with dialog, "It was sweet of you to call me 'Grandmother,' Jeff/Julie. But you know that I am your mother."

- Character B can accept the incorrect relationship created by Character A. Play the rest of the scene in the new role that Character A has created for Character B.

WORKSHOP SIX: SPONTANEITY

Objectives: (1) Participants learn to make rapid adjustments during improvised scene work to accommodate new information, new characters, or a shift in motives.

(2) Participants discover fresh situations through the imposition of sudden transformations.

(3) Participants develop a sense of teamwork and sharing in the process of solving new problems.

Duration: 4 days

Improvisational Exercises:

Word Charades

Sound and Motion Warm-Ups

Abstract Machines

Adding Characters & Shifting Motives

Transformations: Becoming Unfrozen

One Word Motives: Repeat

Suggested Spolin game: Drawing Objects Game

ONE Before the first session of Workshop Six, post the three workshop objectives on the blackboard or bulletin board. These objectives remain on display until the beginning of Workshop Seven.

TWO Actors must be prepared for the unexpected. Actors need to develop the confidence that they can respond in character when performing on-stage with others.

THREE Through improvisation students sharpen their spontaneous responses. Students learn the skills of thinking and reacting naturally without rehearsal. These skills are necessary for the stage as well as for life. Workshop Six concentrates on developing spontaneity.

FOUR "Word Charades" is mentioned in the *Student Handbook* as a warm-up activity for Workshop Six. This exercise encourages participants to think and react spontaneously.

FIVE Refer to Unit One, Workshop Three for complete directions to "Word Charades." The words for this game are reprinted in the Appendix of this text.

SIX Only the procedure for "Word Charades" is described in the *Student Handbook*. None of the card information is included in the student text.

SEVEN Use the remaining "Word Charades" cards for this game. If you used all six sets of cards in Workshop Three, you may wish to create your own new word cards.

> *Actors need to develop the confidence that they can respond in character when performing on-stage with others.*

ACTIVITY #1
Warm-Up Exercises

Purpose:

Actors learn to make rapid adjustments, discover fresh situations, and develop teamwork.

Execution:

ONE Before the first session of Workshop Six, post the three workshop objectives on the blackboard or bulletin board. These objectives remain on display until the beginning of Workshop Seven.

TWO WARM-UP ACTIVITIES: The purpose of a warm-up activity is to warm up the minds and bodies of the participants and to sharpen their responses. During Workshop Six, you may wish to use previously effective warm-up exercises, such as "Zeke-Zork" and "Who Started the Motion."

THREE Only one or two warm-ups are necessary on any single day. Avoid the danger of getting so involved in the warm-ups that there is insufficient time to explore the more complex exercises discussed in Workshops Six and Seven.

FOUR Pick and choose from the following warm-up activities that follow. It is not necessary to use all of the activities at this time.

FIVE WORD CHARADES: This activity is recommended as a warm-up in the *Student Handbook*. "Word Charades" encourages participants to make spontaneous adjustments in fresh situations.

SIX The cards for this game are reprinted only in the Appendix of this book. Please remove the perforated pages and use the cards. The *Student Handbook* does not contain any of the "Word Charades" game cards. Only the exercise objectives and the procedure appear in the *Student Handbook*.

SEVEN SOUND AND MOTION WARM-UPS: This exercise is an excellent warm-up activity. It is described in detail in the *Student Handbook*. "Sound and Motion Warm-Ups" reinforces the following Workshop Six learning objectives:

- Participants learn to make rapid adjustments during improvised scene work to accommodate new information.

- Participants develop a sense of teamwork and sharing.

EIGHT ABSTRACT MACHINES: This exercise is also an effective warm-up activity. "Abstract Machines" is described in detail in the *Student Handbook*. It reinforces the following Workshop Six learning objectives:

- Participants learn to make rapid adjustments during improvised scene work to accommodate new information.

- Participants develop a sense of teamwork and sharing.

"Word Charades" encourages participants to make spontaneous adjustments in fresh situations.

NINE DRAWING OBJECTS GAME: This Spolin exercise is an energetic warm-up activity. The "Drawing Objects Game" challenges the main participants as well as his/her teammates. The "Drawing Objects Game" encourages participants to develop a sense of teamwork and sharing.

The "Drawing Objects Game" challenges the main participants as well as his/her teammates.

ACTIVITY #2

Adding Characters and Shifting Motives

Purpose:

Actors learn to make rapid adjustments, discover fresh situations, and develop teamwork.

Preparation:

ONE ADDING CHARACTERS AND SHIFTING MOTIVES: This activity is one of the seven original Engelsman Theatre Games. The four situations and the twenty-four character cards are printed in the Appendix of this book. In addition, this *Teacher's Guide* provides a thorough explanation of "Adding Characters and Shifting Motives" in the following lesson.

TWO The *Student Handbook* does not include any of the Engelsman Theatre Game Cards.

THREE Prior to Activity #2, divide your class into groups of six. Record the names of students in each group. Once again, try to mix experienced or confident actors with shy or reluctant actors. By creating diversity in each group, students build on each other's strengths.

FOUR On the day of the activity, one team performs at a time. The remaining groups become the audience.

FIVE This activity provides ample opportunities for students to learn, to be creative, and to laugh. Prior to the day you introduce "Adding Characters and Shifting Motives," familiarize yourself with the procedure for playing this game. It is outlined in Activity #2 below. Preplanning saves time and ensures the success of the exercise.

SIX The game offers four different situations. All situations involve six characters. Therefore, for each scene, you will produce cards for Characters A, B, C, D, E, and F. Remove the game card pages. Then cut the cards along the dotted line.

■ SEVEN ■ Give each participant a card on the day that "Adding Characters and Shifting Motives" is played.

Execution:

■ ONE ■ ADDING CHARACTERS AND SHIFTING MOTIVES: This activity is one of the seven original Engelsman Theatre Games. All twenty-four cards for "Adding Characters and Shifting Motives" are printed in the Appendix of this text. The *Student Handbook* prints only the exercise objectives and the procedure for this game.

■ TWO ■ The game "Adding Characters and Shifting Motives" reinforces the following Workshop Six learning objectives:

- Participants learn to make rapid adjustments during improvised scene work to accommodate new information, new characters, or a shift in motives.

- Participants develop a sense of teamwork and sharing in the process of solving new problems.

■ THREE ■ This exercise contains four different situations. Each of the four situations focuses on carefully crafted shifting motives. In each scene, there are six characters. Therefore, you have six character cards for each situation — Characters A, B, C, D, E, and F.

■ FOUR ■ Divide the class into teams of six players. One team performs at a time. The other teams become the audience. The six performers will be given individual cards explaining *where* they are, *who* they are, and *what* their characters want.

Characters should not look at each other's cards or preplan the scene in any way.

■ FIVE ■ All of the Character F cards require the performers to choose their own *who* and *what*. Character F is the only person of the six characters who has this flexility. Characters should not look at each other's cards or preplan the scene in any way. Players will enter one at a time or in pairs as coached by the instructor.

■ SIX ■ Character A enters first. Later he/she is followed by Characters B, C, D, E, and F. Character A begins the scene by establishing *where* the action takes place. He/she strongly suggests *who* he/she is. His/her actions may also suggest what motives are strongest in her mind at the moment the scene begins.

■ SEVEN ■ When Character B enters the scene, he/she should use dialog and actions to establish how he/she knows, or is related to, Character A. Character B also has a *what*. He may urge Character A to help him with his need.

EIGHT Character A should accept the new information that Character B introduces. Character A may ask questions. She can either join Character B and pursue a new motive or ignore Character B's needs. Character B also must adapt to information that Character A adds or reveals while creating dialog.

NINE As the next four characters enter, further adaptation and acceptance of new information will be necessary. Identity cards for Characters C, D, E explain *who* they are and *what* their motives are. The new information they introduce will influence the motives of everyone already on-stage.

Character F must choose his own *who* and *what*. Character F has the responsibility of ending the scene. All six performers should work toward bringing the improvisation to a logical conclusion shortly after Character F's entrance.

TEN Again, there is some ego risk in performing these scenes in front of other classmates. Initially, you may want to rely on more self-confident volunteers to demonstrate this improvisational exercise. Allow potentially shy class members to hold back and observe if they wish. However, quickly encourage them to get involved.

Allow potentially shy class members to hold back and observe if they wish. However, quickly encourage them to get involved.

If a particular scene does not work, be supportive of the actors. Acknowledge that the impasse is partly the nature of improvisation. Sometimes the motives work together beautifully, at other times they do not.

ACTIVITY #3

Improvisational Games

Purpose:

Actors learn to make rapid adjustments, discover fresh situations, and develop teamwork.

Execution:

ONE TRANSFORMATIONS: This activity is described in detail in the *Student Handbook*. This exercise reinforces the following Workshop Six learning objectives:

  • Participants discover fresh situations through the imposition of sudden transformations.

> *"Transformations" is worth repeating on successive days. It is a fine exercise for developing spontaneity.*

• Participants develop a sense of teamwork and sharing.

TWO "Transformations" is worth repeating on successive days. It is a fine exercise for developing spontaneity. Participants enjoy this activity tremendously. Some situations can get silly. Others, however, are a delight.

THREE If actors are unable to create a scene, the teacher can shout FREEZE! Ask a remaining participant to enter the scene with a change in *who*, *where*, and *what*. If the remaining players seem confused, you may need to enter the scene yourself.

FOUR As participants develop confidence, introduce variations and restrictions to make the transformations more challenging. One can vary the game by announcing new categories for the next transformation, such as robots, animals, politicians, children, in an art museum, in a zoo, at a fire, at the South Pole, save the victim, and catch the suspect. To end this activity, state to participants "Only one minute to end the scene."

FIVE "One Word Motives" originally was introduced and described in detail in Workshop Five. This exercise reinforces the following Workshop Six learning objectives:

- • Participants learn to make adjustments during improvised scene work to accommodate their motives.

- • Participants develop spontaneity and a sense of teamwork and sharing.

SIX In Workshop Six students experience more success with "One Word Motives" after they have participated in previous exercises emphasizing spontaneity. Participants now exhibit more self-confidence than they displayed when this game was introduced in Workshop Five.

WORKSHOP SEVEN: MORE COMPLEX IMPROVISATIONS

Objectives: (1) Participants learn the problems that a director and actors experience when many performers are on-stage at the same time.

(2) Participants discover how to give a scene focus by learning to *give* and *take*.

(3) Participants develop a sense of ensemble acting.

(4) Participants learn to stay in character.

Duration: 3 days

Improvisational Exercises:

> *Sound and Motion Give and Take*
>
> *Christmas Rush*
>
> *International Airport*

Suggested Spolin game: Two Scenes

ONE Before the first sessions of Workshop Seven, post the four workshop objectives on the blackboard or bulletin board. These objectives remain on display until the conclusion of Workshop Seven.

TWO Workshop Seven is the culmination of the two units on improvisation. This text has covered only a portion of the improvisational techniques and exercises available for teachers.

THREE Instructors could spend an entire year on improvisational exercises alone. However, most teachers devote only a few weeks or months to this aspect of theatre education. Why? Theatre education is multifaceted. Each facet stresses and teaches important skills.

FOUR At the completion of Workshop Seven students will have acquired a degree of competency and sophistication in their performances. Participants will have acquired numerous skills which they can apply to other aspects of theatre education. Can the group work as an ensemble? Does the group

Theatre education is multifaceted. Each facet stresses and teaches important skills.

"Christmas Rush" and "International Airport" enable students to utilize the skills that they have learned in earlier workshops.

use pantomime effectively? Have the students learned the concept of *give* and *take?* Do participants show an awareness of how dramatic conflict builds? Workshop Seven answers these questions.

FIVE During this workshop students are asked to create two complex scenes, "Christmas Rush" and "International Airport." Both exercises involve many characters on-stage at the same time. Both "Christmas Rush" and "International Airport" involve humor and require students to think and act spontaneously. "Christmas Rush" and "International Airport" enable students to utilize the skills that they have learned in earlier workshops.

SIX If the scenes in these two activities work, Bravo! If they do not, you might analyze what went wrong, try the activities a second time, consider "Christmas Rush" and "International Airport" a challenging experiment, and acknowledge that the group could use more experience with improvised scenes.

SEVEN CHRISTMAS RUSH and INTERNATIONAL AIRPORT are two of the seven original Engelsman Theatre Games. The twelve "Christmas Rush" character/situation cards and the fifteen "International Airport" character name cards are printed in the Appendix of this text. In addition, this *Teacher's Guide* provides a thorough explanation for these games.

EIGHT Information contained on the individual cards for "Christmas Rush" and "International Airport" is not included in the *Student Handbook*. The *Student Handbook* prints only the exercise objectives and the procedure for this game.

ACTIVITY #1

Sound and Motion Give and Take

Purpose:

Actors discover how to give a scene focus by learning to give and take.

Execution:

ONE Before the first session of Workshop Seven, post the four workshop objectives on the blackboard or bulletin board. These objectives remain on display until the conclusion of Workshop Seven.

TWO WARM-UP ACTIVITIES: The purpose of a warm-up activity is to warm up the minds and bodies of the participants and to sharpen their responses.

THREE SOUND AND MOTION GIVE AND TAKE: This is an energetic warm-up. It is described in detail in the *Student Handbook*. Review this description. Be prepared to introduce the exercise to your students. This improvisational activity encourages participants to learn to focus a scene through the process of give and take.

FOUR "Sound and Motion Give and Take" provides an enjoyable educational activity. Learning to *give* and *take* is a necessary skill not only for stage but also in daily life. "Sound and Motion Give and Take" elevates the energy level of the participants and prepares the group for the next two exercises.

FIVE Spolin's "Two Scenes" provides a fine introduction to giving and taking in scene work. Play this game prior to the "Christmas Rush" activity. Students are better prepared for Activity #2 when they first participate in Spolin's "Two Scenes." This exercise helps give a scene focus by learning to give and take.

> *Learning to give and take is a necessary skill not only for stage but also in daily life.*

ACTIVITY #2
Christmas Rush

Purpose:

Actors discover how to give a scene focus by learning to give and take.

Preparation:

ONE CHRISTMAS RUSH: This activity is one of the seven original Engelsman Theatre Games. All twelve character/situation "Christmas Rush" cards are reprinted in the Appendix of this text. In addition, a thorough explanation of the game "Christmas Rush" follows.

TWO The *Student Handbook* does not include any of the Engelsman Theatre Game Cards.

THREE The activity has twelve cards. There is one card for each of the twelve characters. All twelve character roles are interchangeable for males and females. All twelve characters are given a card before the improvisation begins. They do not share the information on their individual cards with one another.

FOUR The teacher needs to prepare cards to hand to each participant on the day "Christmas Rush" is played. Twelve character cards, describing the *who, where,* and *what,* are reprinted in the Appendix of this text. All twelve character roles are interchangeable for males and females. All twelve characters are given a card before the improvisation begins. They do not share the information on their individual cards with one another.

Execution:

ONE CHRISTMAS RUSH reinforces the following Workshop Seven learning objectives:

Participants learn the problems a director and actors face when a large number of people are on-stage at one time.

- Participants learn the problems a director and actors face when a large number of people are on-stage at one time.

- Students learn to give a scene focus by learning to give and take.

- Students develop a sense of ensemble acting.

- Students learn to stay in character.

TWO The activity has twelve cards. There is one card for each of the twelve characters.

THREE Hand the prepared cards to each actor on the day "Christmas Rush" is played. All twelve character roles are interchangeable for males and females. All twelve characters are given a card before the improvisation begins. Performers do not share the information on their individual cards with one another.

FOUR Assign twelve volunteers a role by handing each a card. Explain that the scene is a local post office at Christmas time.

FIVE Eight characters will be on-stage when the scene begins. Characters #5, #10, #11, and #12 are off-stage. They will enter as the scene develops. Their cards explain when they should arrive.

SIX The following diagram displays furniture arrangement for a post office interior. The instructor and performers should feel free to alter this plan, but it is important that all participants know the layout of the post office set before this improvisation begins.

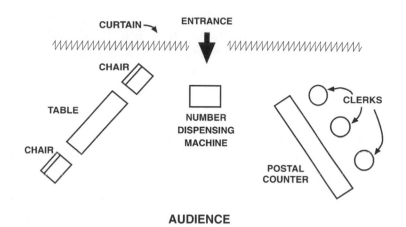

SEVEN When you signal the start of the scene, Character #1 and Character #6 capture the initial focus with their improvised dialog. After that, it may be difficult to predict how the scene will develop. You have diverse characters, each with a unique need and motive. All performers need to practice the skills of give and take.

You have diverse characters, each with a unique need and motive.

EIGHT Each actor enacts his/her character's need for being at the post office. Actors must decide when their character logically should leave the scene. Once a character departs, he does not return.

This is a complex improvisation. Actors do not have to unify or resolve all conflicts at the end of the exercise.

NINE CHRISTMAS RUSH — Steps for success:

• Provide tables and chairs to represent counter surfaces and to define the interior limits of the post office. One chair may be used to represent the number dispensing machine near the door.

• Use a follow spotlight or a large flashlight to establish where the audience and actors should focus their attention. The instructor or a nonperforming student shines the light on a portion of the stage. The high-lighted actors must speak loudly. They must develop the *who* and the *what* on their cards.

• Focus first on Clerk #1 and his/her customer, number 73. Maintain the focus on these two actors for a minute. As the spotlight moves from one section of the post office to another, give the newly featured players a chance to develop a relationship or a conflict. Hold the spotlight on them until the scene loses force.

- When the spotlight shifts to another group, the first actors may continue talking. But they should lower their voices to an undertone. The first actors can pantomime their conversations. Later they can come alive again with normal speech whenever the spotlight focuses on them.

- Resist the temptation to move the spotlight around the room bringing dormant characters to life. Slowly, some of the performers will learn to take the scene. If they succeed in their attempts, feature them with the spotlight.

- Actors should not feel that they must stay in one place on-stage. Some should move around the set. Other performers will be more in character if they stay in one area.

- Performers can pantomime characters' clothing and props. However, simple props add interest, humor, realism, and excitement to "Christmas Rush." Therefore, you may wish to provide:

  A variety of hats for characters to use;

  A clipboard for Character #4;

  Twelve packages for Character #7;

  Some unwrapped items (no boxes) and some brown paper and tape for Character #10.

- If possible, the instructor or a nonperforming student could videotape this improvisation. Then the group can view the scene upon completion. You also can analyze those factors that worked well and those areas that need improvement.

TEN DISCUSSING THE SCENE AT THE COMPLETION OF THE "CHRISTMAS RUSH" ACTIVITY.

A. At the close of "Christmas Rush," analyze those factors that worked well and those areas that need improvement. To provide focus for the discussion, precede the questions with the following statement: "Christmas Rush" has provided you, the actor, the opportunity to understand the problems that a director and other actors experience when many performers are on-stage at the same time. You learned to *give* and *take*. You learned to stay in character. These are skills that you will need as an actor.

You learned to give and take. You learned to stay in character. These are skills that you will need as an actor.

B. Begin by noting the successful actions and dialog of several actors. Note particular moments when the focus was clear. Note times when the performers seemed to be in character. Recall examples of humorous dialog and action.

C. Questions to ask the group:

- Were the humorous moments and actions appropriate?

- Can you give examples of divided focus?

- When, if ever, did the scene begin to slow down?

- How could you improve this scene?

D. Remember to keep the comments positive. Do not allow personal attacks on actors.

E. Solutions to problems should be ensemble solutions.

F. If students enjoyed this exercise, "Christmas Rush" can be repeated with new actors. Encourage the new cast to invent fresh interpretive actions.

> *Remember to keep the comments positive. Do not allow personal attacks on actors.*

ACTIVITY #3

International Airport

Purpose:

Actors discover how to give a scene focus by learning to give and take.

Preparation:

ONE "International Airport" is one of the seven original Engelsman Theatre Games. Fifteen "International Airport" cards are printed in the Appendix of this book. In addition, a thorough explanation of this game is printed in the following "International Airport" lesson plan.

TWO The *Student Handbook* does not include the "International Airport" cards, the fact sheet, or the public address announcements. The *Student Handbook* prints only the exercise objectives and the procedure for this game.

THREE The activity requires fifteen cards. There is one card for each of the fifteen characters. The teacher needs to give each participant a card on the day that "International Airport" is played.

FOUR This improvisational exercise is similar in focus and intent to "Christmas Rush." "International Airport" is an activity that involves many players on-stage at one time. For student success, you may wish to have a student read the script for the public address announcements.

FIVE All fifteen character cards are printed in the Appendix of this text. In addition, this Appendix provides a fact sheet, which you may wish to use with this activity. A student or the instructor can create a third optional item — a tape recording of the airport public address announcements. This item lends realism to the scene. However, a participant can read the script from the side of the stage.

SIX When you assign roles to actors, give preference to students who did not perform in "Christmas Rush."

SEVEN The fact sheet can be found in the Appendix.

EIGHT A text of the airport public address announcements can be found in the Appendix. An actor may read the airport public address announcements from the side of the stage. Or a student or instructor can prerecord the announcements prior to playing this activity.

The airport public address announcement script was written for a Midwestern airport. Each participant on-stage during the "International Airport" improvisation should regard the announcements as part of the waiting room environment.

- Each actor should react in character if the loudspeaker announces a name, flight number or destination, that he/she has included in his/her fact sheet.

- An actor should react indifferently if the announcement has nothing to do with information on his/her fact sheet.

- If a character has already left the scene or if the character has not yet arrived at the airport, the actor should not respond to an individual page.

- Actors should continue developing an improvised dialog with another character even though the announcement may have interrupted that dialog.

- Each actor may use any announcement as a motive for a response or action of some sort. However, such reactions should be limited to one or, at the most, two reactions per improvisation.

Actors should continue developing an improvised dialog with another character even though the announcement may have interrupted that dialog.

Execution:

ONE INTERNATIONAL AIRPORT: This exercise reinforces and focuses on the following Workshop Seven learning objectives:

- Participants learn the problems a director and actors face when a large number of people are on-stage at one time.

- Students learn to give a scene focus by learning to give and take.

- Students develop a sense of ensemble acting.

- Students learn to stay in character.

> *Students develop a sense of ensemble acting. Students learn to stay in character.*

TWO Like the "Christmas Rush" activity, "International Airport" has a suggested ground plan. Chairs and tables are arranged to help define the waiting room area. Remember to leave space for the exits. The following diagram displays the arrangement of furniture for an airport waiting room. Feel free to alter this plan. It is important that all participants know the layout of your airport set before this improvisation begins.

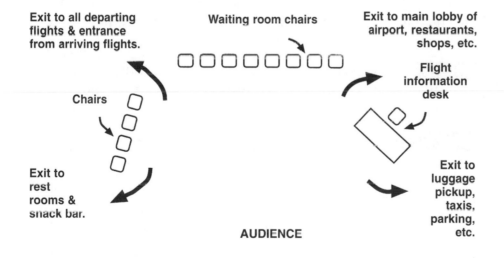

THREE You can increase the players' sense of security by providing props like hats, luggage, garment bags, cameras, tennis rackets, backpacks, purses, and other carryon bags. These items, however, may be pantomimed.

FOUR When choosing actors, give preference to students who did not perform in "Christmas Rush." Then have each of the selected actors take one character card, at random. Next, give each character a fact sheet which you have prepared prior to class. After receiving a character card, each actor fills out the fact sheet.

An example of a profile fact sheet is provided in the Preparation Ideas for Activity #3. This profile fact sheet allows the actor to choose individual characteristics for the person he/she portrays.

FIVE Tell participants that anyone who draws the last name *Hedley* or *Nelson* needs to ask if anyone else has drawn the same last names. Those actors should decide on a relationship for each character such as mother, father, husband, wife, child, grandchild, grandmother, or aunt. They also need to decide if they are traveling together or if one is meeting the other. These players need to compare fact sheets. However, this is the only preplanning that takes place.

SIX Appoint one or two flight information attendants. Airport personnel do not need to complete the information on the fact sheet.

SEVEN If "International Airport" is repeated several times, a "live" announcer may wish to improvise his/her own announcements. The actor can use flight numbers that appear on the fact sheet. The public address announcement script might then serve as a model.

EIGHT Once everyone has read the instructions, filled out a fact sheet, and clarified any questions about procedure, the improvisation begins.

Look about you. Notice others. Do not feel that you must start a conversation or develop a conflict.

NOTE

Stay in character. If your character prefers to remain quiet and isolated, remain quiet and isolated. Look about you. Notice others. Do not feel that you must start a conversation or develop a conflict. You are in a waiting room. How does your character behave while waiting? Consider *taking* the scene if it fits your character to do so. Also be prepared to *give*. Share. Strive for focus. Share the scene with the audience. If the focus is on you, be sure you can be seen and heard. Stay in character.

NINE The instructor should inject side-coaching comments only when they might seem to help. When you sense that the scene is drawing to a close, you can announce, "One minute left. Wrap it up in one minute. Thirty seconds left. CURTAIN!" Most likely, though, the improvisation will conclude before the tape recorded announcements end.

TEN Videotaping this activity is an excellent learning device. Whether or not you videotape "International Airport," discuss those factors that worked well and those areas that need improvement. Read the following discussion session. It is identical to the discussion that you used after "Christmas Rush."

ELEVEN DISCUSSING THE SCENE AT THE COMPLETION OF "INTERNATIONAL AIRPORT" ACTIVITY

A. At the close of "International Airport," analyze those factors that worked well and those areas that need improvement. To provide focus for the discussion, precede the questions with the following statement:

"International Airport" has provided you, the actor, the opportunity to understand the problems that a director and other actors experience when many performers are on-stage at the same time. You learned to *give* and *take*. You learned to stay in character. These are skills that you will need as an actor.

B. Begin by noting the successful actions and dialog of several actors. Note particular moments when the focus was clear. Note times when the performers seemed to be in character. Recall examples of humorous dialog and action.

C. Questions to ask the group:

• Were the humorous moments and actions appropriate?

• Can you give examples of divided focus?

• When, if ever, did the scene begin to slow down?

• How could you improve this scene?

D. Remember to keep the comments positive. Do not allow personal attacks on actors.

E. Solutions to problems should be ensemble solutions.

F. If students enjoyed this exercise, "International Airport" can be repeated with new actors. Encourage the new cast to invent fresh interpretive actions.

At the close of "International Airport," analyze those factors that worked well and those areas that need improvement.

TAKING A LOOK AHEAD

Although it seems as if the semester has just begun, it is time to take a look ahead to the end of the semester. Unit Seven in the *Student Handbook* describes the end-of-semester project. Take time now to read Unit Seven before you discuss the program possibilities with the class.

Theatre is a performing art. Theatre people have a goal. That goal is to communicate feelings and ideas to their audience. Therefore, it is natural for a theatre class to combine its talents and present a final performance. This final project is similar to a chorus or orchestra concert.

Looking ahead to the end-of-semester project has several advantages. First, students recognize the fuller picture of the overall objectives of the *Student Handbook*. Secondly, participants begin to direct their attention to the multifaceted roles they might play during the end-of-semester project.

The instructor needs to make several decisions now regarding:

- The amount of time you wish to spend on this class project,

- The date and time of the performance, and

- The place where you will give the performance.

In addition, you and your class will have to choose the type of production and performance the class will offer, and the audience that you will be serving. After you have familiarized yourself with Unit Seven, devote a class period to discussions regarding the kind of performance the group would like to offer. Although students have been in class only six to eight weeks, the end of the semester arrives quickly. Students have to be prepared for the project.

> *You [the instructor] need to assess whether or not you have students who have the interest, talent, and leadership qualities to be effective directors.*

Will you, the instructor, choose a single play that you will direct? Or will you encourage students to try their hand at directing? You need to assess whether or not you have students who have the interest, talent, and leadership qualities to be effective directors. If you do not have a student with the proper qualities, your task is simplified. You will direct a play or an act from a play that can include everybody — or almost everybody — in a role.

Pick three or four possible selections from which students can choose in the next few weeks. Spend a class period now having students read out loud the opening pages in Unit Seven of the *Student Handbook*. Read the pages even though you do not plan to teach the unit for several weeks. If students wish to self direct this project, recruit directors, prop persons, and set designers now.

If you choose the less stressful option of directing and working with a single script, you still need to consider the play you will produce. Following are several suggestions for you to preview.

If students wish to self-direct this project, recruit directors, prop persons, and set designers now.

PLAYS SUITABLE FOR ELEMENTARY SCHOOL AUDIENCES

Numerous play collections (Contemporary Drama Service/ Meriwether Publishing Ltd.).

Story Theatre by Paul Sills (Samuel French).

The Nose Tree by Alan Engelsman found in *Theatre Arts I Student Handbook* (Contemporary Drama Service/Meriwether Publishing Ltd.).

The Canterbury Tales adapted by Bernice Bronson (New Plays, Inc.).

PLAYS WITH LARGE CASTS

Numerous play collections (Contemporary Drama Service/ Meriwether Publishing Ltd.).

Voices From the High School by Peter Dee (Baker's Plays).

Act III of *The Crucible* by Arthur Miller (Dramatists Play Service).

Act III of *The Skin of Our Teeth* by Thornton Wilder (Samuel French).

Act II of *Inherit the Wind* by Lawrence and Lee (Dramatists Play Service).

CUTTINGS FROM SHAKESPEARE

Julius Caesar, Taming of the Shrew, Romeo and Juliet, A Midsummer Night's Dream.

An important question to ask yourself is, "Can I complete Units Three, Four, Five, and Six and still have time left in the semester for an end-of-semester project?" If not, decide how you can shorten the lesson plans over the next several weeks so that you have more time at the end of the semester. One possibility would be to omit one of the units in its entirety. You could complete the omitted unit during the next semester.

UNIT SUMMARY

Unit Two introduced actors to sounds and dialog in improvisational exercises.

Unit One introduced participants to improvisational theatre activities. Actors learned to interact with other performers and to communicate in pantomime. Unit Two introduced actors to sounds and dialog in improvisational exercises. Students completed four new workshops and learned fifteen skills in Unit Two. The four improvisational workshops you completed were titled: *Sound and Motion, Integrating "Who," "Where," and "What," Spontaneity,* and *More Complex Improvisations.*

Following is a list of fifteen skills participants learned in this unit:

1. Strengthened memory and listening skills.

2. Learned to respond rapidly to nonverbal symbols.

3. Experimented with the range and power of vocal expressions.

4. Used movement to enhance communication.

5. Explored nonverbal aspects of speech (such as pitch, tone, and facial expression) to add meaning to language.

6. Reinforced the concepts of *where* and *who* in rudimentary scene work which incorporates both pantomime and speech.

7. Developed scenes containing dramatic conflict.

8. Introduced a *what,* a motive.

9. Learned to make rapid adjustments during improvised scene work to accommodate new information, new characters, or a shift in motives.

10. Discovered fresh situations through the imposition of sudden transformations.

11. Developed a sense of teamwork and sharing in the process of solving new problems.

12. Learned the problems that a director and actors experience when many performers are on-stage at the same time.

13. Discovered how to give a scene focus by learning to *give* and *take*.

14. Developed a sense of ensemble acting.

15. Learned to stay in character.

[Participants] developed a sense of ensemble acting.

Voice Control and Oral Interpretation

In Unit One and Unit Two students experienced dramatic movement and speech without scripts. Students developed skills in a relaxed, game-like atmosphere. Unit Three introduces students to the short script. The *Student Handbook* clearly defines the purpose of each activity. Moreover, specific directions and procedural steps for each exercise are included in the student text.

Utilizing a combination of short scripts and poetry, Unit Three introduces new skills and offers participants the opportunity to make educated choices. In this unit students develop twelve skills. Four of the twelve competencies that students develop are:

- Participants gain experience in oral expression by recording a radio commercial.

- Participants gain skills by tape recording a soap opera.

- Students develop skills and experience as they prepare short poems for oral interpretation.

- Participants learn how to mark a script for oral interpretation.

The complete list of learned skills appears at the end of this unit in the summary.

Following are three weekly calendars summarizing each day's activities. The calendar format is provided for your convenience so that you can quickly review each week's activities ahead of time; or give a copy of your weekly syllabus to your principal or department chairperson.

Students develop skills and experience as they prepare short poems for oral interpretation.

UNIT THREE: VOICE CONTROL AND ORAL INTERPRETATION

MONDAY	TUESDAY	WEDNESDAY	THURSDAY	FRIDAY
DAY ONE *ACTIVITY #1* *EXERCISE A* (1) Read aloud page one of Unit Three. (2) Demonstrate "Cuddles" — a radio commercial. Select four students to read commercial. (3) Involve class in script analysis of "Cuddles." Read commentary and questions in the *Student Handbook*. (4) Divide class into five or six groups. Give each student a focus form for recording a commercial. (5) Lastly, each group chooses a director and character roles.	*DAY TWO* *ACTIVITY #1* *EXERCISE A* (1) Continue "Cuddles" commercial." Students break into their groups. (2) Each group records the "Cuddles" commercial" several times. Determine if one recording is better than the other. (3) Groups reconvene. (4) Lastly, randomly choose two groups to play recordings of their commercials.	*DAY THREE* *ACTIVITY #1* *EXERCISE B* (1) Divide class into five or six groups. (2) Give each student a copy of the focus form for recording a commercial. (3) Students record commercial "Mr. Piddley." (4) Students complete and return the focus form to the teacher at the end of the activity. (5) In the last ten minutes of class, randomly choose two groups to play the best recordings of the "Mr. Piddley" commercial.	*DAY FOUR* *ACTIVITY #1* *EXERCISE C* (1) Divide class into five or six groups. (2) Give each student a copy of focus form for recording a commercial. (3) Students record the commercial "Rusty Jones." (4) Students complete and return the focus form to the teacher at the end of the activity. (5) In the last ten minutes of class, randomly choose two groups to play the best recordings of the "Rusty Jones" commercial.	*DAY FIVE* *ACTIVITY #2* *EXERCISE A* (1) Have students read out loud the explanation of Activity #2 in the *Student Handbook*. (2) Then read "Preparation for Taping Soap Operas" out loud. (3) Select five students to demonstrate recording techniques. (4) Instructor models director's role using the first segment of "Lexington Heights." (5) Divide class into two or three groups. (6) Give each student a copy of the focus form for recording a soap opera.

WEEK AT A GLANCE: WEEK ONE

UNIT THREE: VOICE CONTROL AND ORAL INTERPRETATION

MONDAY	TUESDAY	WEDNESDAY	THURSDAY	FRIDAY
DAY SIX *ACTIVITY #2* *EXERCISE A* (1) Continue Activity #2. (2) Students work on their recordings for the soap opera "Lexington Heights." (3) Students coordinate sound effects with script. (4) Students complete the focus form. They return the forms to the teacher at the conclusion of the exercise.	*DAY SEVEN* *ACTIVITY #2* *EXERCISE A* (1) Students continue recording the soap opera "Lexington Heights." (2) By the end of the period each group will have a finished recording of "Lexington Heights" with sound effects. (3) Team members complete their focus sheets. (4) Each group discusses the best segments of their recorded soap opera when they reconvene in the last twenty minutes. (5) Each team plays a recording of the best segment.	*DAY EIGHT* *ACTIVITY #3* *EXERCISE A* (1) Students read out loud introductory material "Oral Interpretation" from the *Student Handbook*. (2) Next, read orally ten "Tips for Preparing an Oral Presentation." (3) Read section titled "Marking a Script for Oral Interpretation." (4) Instructor demonstrates marking a script for oral interpretation. Give each student a copy of nursery rhyme #2. (5) Students mark rhyme for speaking.	*DAY NINE* *ACTIVITY #3* *EXERCISE B* (1) Give each student a copy of the sheet "Marking a Script for Oral Interpretation." Students write "School Lunch" on lines and mark poem for oral presentation. (2) In addition, give each student a focus form you created for this exercise. Collect the form at the end of the activity. (3) Divide class into five or six groups. (4) Students have twenty-five minutes to prepare a group reading of the poem. (5) Groups reconvene. Choose two groups to present or play recordings of the poem.	*DAY TEN* *ACTIVITY #4* *EXERCISE A* (1) Begin Activity #4. (2) Give each student a copy of the sheet "Marking a Script for Oral Interpretation." Students write the poem "Where Are the Words?" on lines and mark the poem for oral presentation. (3) Divide class into groups. (4) Students have twenty-five minutes to prepare individual readings of the poem. (5) Groups reconvene. Choose two groups to present or play recordings of the poem.

WEEK AT A GLANCE: WEEK TWO

UNIT THREE: VOICE CONTROL AND ORAL INTERPRETATION

MONDAY	TUESDAY	WEDNESDAY	THURSDAY	FRIDAY
DAY ELEVEN *ACTIVITY #4* *EXERCISE B* (1) Continue Activity #3. (2) Give each student a copy of the sheet "Marking a Script for Oral Interpretation." Students write "Dog Days" on lines and mark the poem for oral interpretation. (3) Divide class into groups. (4) Students have twenty-five minutes to prepare individual readings of the poem. Reluctant learners can prepare a group reading. (5) Groups reconvene. Choose two groups to present or play recordings of the poem.	*DAY TWELVE* *ACTIVITY #4* *EXERCISE C* (1) Continue Activity #3. (2) Give each student a copy of the sheet "Marking a Script for Oral Interpretation." Students write "Rap Poem" on lines and mark rap for oral presentation. (3) Divide class into groups. (4) Students have twenty-five minutes to prepare individual readings of the poem. Reluctant learners can prepare a group reading. (5) Groups reconvene. Choose two groups to present or play recordings of the poem.	*DAY THIRTEEN* *UNIT REVIEW* *PRACTICE-TALENT* *DAY* (1) Students read aloud the Unit Summary for Unit Three. (2) On the board, write the theatre values listed in the *Teacher's Guide*. (3) Next, ask a student to read aloud the skills learned in Unit Three. Students benefit from reviewing the skills they have learned. (4) Next, discuss Talent Day. Read suggestions in the *Student Handbook*.	*DAY FOURTEEN* *TALENT DAY* (1) Each student will present some performance for the class. (2) Students may give a group or individual presentation. (3) Suggestions for talent day are described at the end of this unit in the *Student Handbook*	*DAY FIFTEEN* *TALENT DAY* (1) Repeat Day Fourteen.

WEEK AT A GLANCE: WEEK THREE

ACTIVITY #1
Radio Commercials

Group Performances

ONE Activity #1 is titled "Recording a Radio Commercial." It emphasizes group performances. The *Student Handbook* contains the entire commercial, "Cuddles," as Exercise A.

TWO Minidramas on radio commercials make ideal first scripts for analysis and interpretation. They are short, contemporary, humorous, and nonthreatening. Students can practice them over and over again. No live audience critiques them on their performance. Students critique themselves. At the conclusion of the taping, the group takes pride in its accomplishments.

THREE Each group needs two tape recorders: one tape recorder for making the recording and a portable CD player or second tape recorder for playing background music and sound effects. Student-owned audio equipment is suitable also.

It is best to accumulate your equipment several days prior to the lesson. In that way, there are few surprises.

Two days before Activity #1, ask six students to bring a tape recorder or CD player. Provide a locked cabinet or closet to store recorders safely overnight. Perhaps your school can provide any additional tape recorders. It is best to accumulate your equipment several days prior to the lesson. In that way, there are few surprises.

FOUR The same planning is required for each of the three exercises.

FIVE Prior to Activity #1, divide your class into groups of four to six students. List the names of students in each group. Once again, mix experienced or confident actors with shy or reluctant actors. Attempt to create comfortable diversity in groups. Students build on each other's strengths.

SIX Some instructors like to separate their groups into different rooms or areas. Other teachers like to keep the groups in one environment where they can see each group on task. You need to choose the best method to meet your needs and the needs of your students and principal.

SEVEN Choose the location where all five or six groups convene at the completion of their recording sessions. The meeting area can be simply the middle of the room. Planning details ahead of time helps students succeed in this activity.

EIGHT Before the class begins, prepare recording stations around the room. Preorganizing the stations saves class time and enables students to begin this activity quickly. Students should consider their station an actual recording studio.

NINE Give each student the following focus form. Students are to complete the information on the sheet as they prepare for their radio commercial, "Cuddles." The form keeps students on task and gives structure, organization, and purpose to the activity. Require each participant to return the completed focus sheet at the end of the activity. The lesson may take two days.

Students should consider their station an actual recording studio.

NAME: _____ DATE:_____

Focus Form for Recording Radio Commercials

Each participant is required to return the completed focus sheet to the instructor at the end of the activity.

ACTIVITY #1: EXERCISE_____

NAME OF COMMERCIAL: _____

1. Choose a director. This person has the final authority regarding casting, interpretation, and sound effects. Everyone in the group must agree on the choice of the director.

    The name of the director is: _____

2. Choose a technical director. This person is responsible for operating the tape recorder and setting up the microphone. If the group is small, the director and technical director may have speaking roles. However, they should be small roles.

    The name of the technical director is: _____

3. Before assigning any speaking roles, ask several actors and actresses to read the same roles. You might even try using females for male roles and males for female roles.

    _____ plays the part of _____

    _____ plays the part of _____

    _____ plays the part of _____

    _____ plays the part of _____

4. Rehearse, tape, and play back. Give helpful comments. Change the way you read the commercial. Then tape again. Which recording is the best? Version #1 _____ Version #2 _____

There are three reasons that Version # _____ is the best.

First, _____

_____

_____

Second, _____

_____

_____

Third, _____

_____

_____

TEN All procedures, forms, and comments are intended as suggestions. Every teacher brings specific strengths, experiences, and interests to class. Adapting a lesson to fit your needs makes the lesson more meaningful to you, the instructor.

Cuddles

Purpose:

Actors gain experience in oral expression by recording a radio commercial.

Execution:

ONE DEMONSTRATION: On the first day of the unit the entire class meets as one group. Arbitrarily assign the parts to four students. In addition to the four speaking parts, select a person to play "Cuddles" and to do other sound effects. Seek imaginative ways of creating the crash effect. You may wish to have a crash box already on hand. In front of the class, the four actors read the script "Cuddles" from Unit Three in the *Student Handbook.*

TWO Next, involve the entire class in a script analysis of the "Cuddles" commercial. Use the commentary and questions that appear in the *Student Handbook.*

THREE Before class begins, prepare recording stations around the room. In each area place a tape recorder. In addition, you may wish to provide a portable CD player or tape recorder for the technical director to use for sound effects. Students should consider their station an actual recording studio.

FOUR Divide the class into five or six groups. Read the names of the students on each team. Assign each group a recording station. Give each student a copy of the Focus Form on page 66 for recording a commercial.

FIVE You may wish to create another Focus Form to better meet your needs. Each participant is required to return the completed focus form to the instructor at the end of the activity. The Unit Three calendar in this *Teacher's Guide* schedules two days for the "Cuddles" activity.

Every teacher brings specific strengths, experiences, and interests to class. Adapting a lesson to fit your needs makes the lesson more meaningful to you, the instructor.

Theatre Arts 1: Teacher's Course Guide

SIX As the teams prepare for recording the radio commercial "Cuddles," each student completes the focus sheet. After each group has recorded the commercial two times, they return to the designated meeting place.

SEVEN Since all of your groups have a diverse population, randomly choose two groups to play the tape of their best version of the commercial. In that way, no group is singled out as more talented.

> *Most people enjoy hearing themselves and their friends on tape.*

EIGHT Then have each team discuss those elements that created the best version of their commercial. Most people enjoy hearing themselves and their friends on tape. During the playback session students will be high-spirited and delight in identifying who is speaking. Sometimes it may be difficult to keep the critique of the recordings focused.

NINE Students need to concentrate on their group's successful interpretation of the script. Note effective pauses, emphases, and inflections. However, the purpose of this activity is to provide an enjoyable oral expression experience. Extensive criticism is not necessary in this exercise.

TEN Assign the commercials, "Mr. Piddley" and "Rusty Jones," to read for homework. These two commercials are located in the Appendix of the *Student Handbook*.

EXERCISE B
Mr. Piddley

Purpose:

Actors gain experience in oral expression by recording a radio commercial.

Execution:

ONE Direct student attention to the radio commercial, "Mr. Piddley," located in the Appendix of the *Student Handbook*.

TWO As in past activities, divide the class into five or six teams. Read the names of the students in each section. Assign each group a recording station. In each area place a tape recorder. In addition, you may wish to provide a tape recorder or portable CD player for the technical director to use for sound effects.

THREE Give every class member a copy of the focus form for recording a commercial. Require each participant to return the completed focus sheet to the instructor at the end of the activity.

FOUR You may wish to create a focus form that better suits your needs. These forms concentrate student attention on the task at hand. Focus sheets make students accountable for their behaviors and help students organize their groups quickly. Focus sheets provide the instructor a description of each person's job.

FIVE As the teams prepare for recording the radio commercial, "Rusty Jones," each student completes the focus sheet. After each group has recorded the commercial two times, they are to return to the designated meeting place.

SIX Next, since all of your groups have a diverse population, randomly choose two groups to play the tape of their best version of the commercial. In that way, no group is singled out as more talented.

SEVEN Each team discusses those elements that created the best version of their commercial. Concentrate students' attention on their group's successful interpretation of the script. Note effective pauses, emphases, and inflections on the recordings. Extensive criticism is not necessary in this exercise.

> *Focus sheets make students accountable for their behaviors and help students organize their groups quickly.*

EXERCISE C
Rusty Jones

Purpose:

Actors gain experience in oral expression by recording a radio commercial.

Execution:

ONE Direct student attention to the radio commercial, "Rusty Jones," located in the Appendix of the *Student Handbook.*

TWO Once again, divide the class into five or six teams. Read the names of the students in each section. Assign each group a recording station. In each area place a tape recorder. In addition, you may wish to provide a tape recorder or portable CD player for the technical director to use for sound effects.

THREE Give every participant on each team a copy of the focus form for recording a commercial. Require each participant to return the completed focus sheet to the instructor at the end of the activity.

FOUR You may wish to create a focus form that better suits your needs. These forms concentrate student attention on the task at hand. Focus sheets make students accountable for their behaviors and help students organize their groups quickly. Focus sheets provide the instructor a description of each person's job.

FIVE As the teams prepare for recording the radio commercial, "Rusty Jones," each student completes the focus sheet. After each group has recorded the commercial two times, they are to return to the designated meeting place.

SIX Next, since all of your groups have a diverse population, randomly choose two groups to play the tape of their best version of the commercial. In that way, no group is singled out as more talented.

SEVEN Each team discusses those elements that created the best version of their commercial. Concentrate students' attention on their group's successful interpretation of the script. Note effective pauses, emphases, and inflections. Extensive criticism is not necessary in this exercise.

ACTIVITY #2

The Soap Opera

ONE Soap opera dramas are great scripts for analysis and interpretation. Segments are relatively short and contemporary. Soap operas often exaggerate familiar family and job related problems and relationships. In addition, soap operas discuss ethical and moral issues. Students like to watch, read, and write soap operas.

Soap opera dramas are great scripts for analysis and interpretation.

The entire soap opera, "Lexington Heights," is located in the Appendix of the *Student Handbook*.

TWO RECORDING A SOAP OPERA: This exercise is a group activity. The *Student Handbook* contains a detailed description of the exercise. "Recording a Soap Opera" encourages participants to practice oral interpretation and voice control.

THREE For both the optional in-class demonstration and the independent work the following day, each group needs two tape recorders: one for making the recording and one for playing background music and sound effects. More sophisticated audio equipment owned by students would be equally suitable.

Gather your equipment several days prior to your lesson. You will save time on the day of the exercise. Provide a locked cabinet or closet to store recorders safely overnight. Your school may be able to provide additional tape records.

FOUR Sound effect tapes are available at the library or record store. To create live sound effects, the teacher and students could assemble various objects like matches, an ashtray, utensils and door handles. Remind students that the *Student Handbook* encourages them to locate their own music and sound effects. Participants are not restricted to using instructor-provided materials.

Remind students that the Student Handbook encourages them to locate their own music and sound effects.

FIVE Prior to class, divide your class into three groups of eight students. There are twelve characters plus an announcer in the soap opera, "Lexington Heights." Some students will have to read two parts. If students need more direction or attention, create smaller groups of four to six people. Then each student will have two parts.

SIX Next, record the names of students in each group. As in Activity #1, mix experienced or confident actors with shy or reluctant actors. Students build on each other's strengths. Create two or three equally balanced groups. Strive to have the same ratio of males and females in each group.

SEVEN Before class begins, prepare recording stations around the room. Preorganizing the stations saves class time and enables students to begin this activity quickly. Students should consider their station an actual recording studio.

EIGHT Prepare a focus form to give to each student. Students complete the information on the sheet as they prepare for their soap opera, "Lexington Heights." Focus sheets make students accountable and enable participants to organize their groups promptly. This type of form provides a description of each person's job. Moreover, focus forms keep students on task, give structure, organization, and purpose to the activity, and enable the instructor to know the role each team person played. Each participant is required to return the completed focus sheet to the instructor at the end of the activity.

NAME: _____ DATE: _____

Focus Sheet for Recording the Soap Opera, "Lexington Heights"

"Lexington Heights" is printed in the Appendix of the *Student Handbook.*

Each participant is required to return this completed focus sheet to the instructor at the end of the activity.

1. Choose a director. This person has the final authority regarding casting, interpretation, and sound effects. Everyone in the group must agree on the choice of the director.

    The name of the director is: _____

2. Choose a technical director. This person is responsible for operating the tape recorder and setting up the microphone. If the group is small, the director and technical director may have speaking roles. However, they should be small roles.

    The name of the technical director is: _____

3. Before assigning any speaking roles, ask several actors and actresses to read the same roles. You might even try using females for male roles and males for female roles.

SEGMENT 1

_____ plays the part of THE ANNOUNCER.

_____ plays the part of THURSTON.

_____ plays the part of DORSEY.

SEGMENT 2

_____ plays the part of MEG.

_____ plays the part of ADAM.

SEGMENT 3

_____ plays the part of COURTNEY.

_____ plays the part of RICKY.

_____ plays the part of ELIZABETH.

SEGMENT 4

_____ plays the part of RUTH.

_____ plays the part of ANNE.

_____ plays the part of BLAKE.

_____ plays the part of MRS. NEWHOUSE.

_____ plays the part of TONY.

4. Rehearse, tape, and play back. Give helpful comments. Change the way you read the soap opera. Then tape again. In which segment of "Lexington Heights" did the actors have the best vocal control and characterization?

Segment #1 _____ Segment #2 _____ Segment #3 _____ Segment #4 _____

These are three reasons that Segment # _____ is the best.

First, _____

_____

_____

Second, _____

_____

_____

Third, _____

_____

_____

NINE Activity #2 groups are larger because there are more characters in the "Lexington Heights" script. Some instructors like to separate their groups into different rooms or areas. Other teachers like to keep the groups in one environment where they can see each group on task. You need to choose the best method to meet your needs and the needs of your students and principal.

TEN Again, choose the place where you want the groups to meet at the completion of their recording sessions. The meeting area can be the middle of the room. Planning and then explaining details to students ahead of time helps students succeed in all activities.

ELEVEN All procedures, forms, and comments are intended as suggestions. Every teacher brings specific strengths, experiences, and interests to class. Adapting a lesson to fit your needs makes the lesson more meaningful to you, the instructor. Schedule more days for this activity if necessary.

TWELVE At this time, direct student attention to the end of Unit Three and Talent Day. On the weekly Unit Three calendars, several days are devoted to Talent Day. Students need to begin to plan now for their individual or group presentations on these days.

> *Planning and then explaining details to students ahead of time helps students succeed in all activities.*

EXERCISE A

Lexington Heights

Purpose:

Actors practice oral interpretation and voice control.

Execution:

ONE On the first day of Exercise A the entire class meets as one group. Take turns reading out loud the detailed explanation of this exercise in the *Student Handbook*.

TWO Continue reading aloud the section titled "Preparation for Taping Soap Operas." Nine specific tips are outlined for a successful soap opera taping. The soap opera, "Lexington Heights," is located in the Appendix of the *Student Handbook*.

During Exercise A students gain experience in ensemble acting. They practice many skills learned in Units One and Two:

• Giving and taking,

• Remaining in character,

• Shifting motives, and

• Creating two-person scenes.

There is no live audience to critique their performance. Students critique themselves. When they finish recording, actors can take pride in their group's accomplishments.

THREE You may wish to introduce the term **ensemble**. Explain that everyone in the group should be made to feel that his/her contribution is valued. Individuals should be supportive of others rather than critical. The group will know how successful it has been. The harmony of the group will be evident in the quality of the final recording they create.

FOUR *Theatre Arts 1* recommends that the instructor demonstrate this exercise before the students begin their recording. Select five students from the class. Appoint one student as sound effects person. Next, select a second participant as technician (someone to operate the tape recorder or video camera). The other three participants will read the roles of announcer, Thurston, and Dorsey. Record the opening scene of "Lexington Heights."

As director, you can model radio techniques. Use hand signals to cue actors. Coordinate technical effects. The demonstration may take a full class period. However, you will establish the standard of quality for each group's finished product.

As director, you can model radio techniques. Use hand signals to cue actors. Coordinate technical effects.

FIVE Once the class begins recording, the suggested time for this activity is three days. The instructor may choose to designate more or less days for this activity. Announce your time schedule at the outset of the exercise. Tell the students specifically when you expect them to complete their project.

SIX Divide the class into two or three teams. Read the names of the students in each section. Assign each group a recording station. In each area place a tape recorder. In addition, you may wish to provide a portable CD player or tape recorder for the technical director to use for sound effects. Students in each group read the "Lexington Heights" script located in the Appendix of the *Student Handbook*.

SEVEN Give each participant on each team a copy of the focus form for recording a soap opera. Or create any focus sheet that meets your needs. Everyone is required to return the completed focus sheet to the instructor at the close of the activity.

Each student completes the form as the team prepares for their group recording of "Lexington Heights." After each team has recorded the soap opera, they return to the designated meeting place.

EIGHT When the class reconvenes, each group discusses those elements that produced the best recorded segments of their soap opera. Most people enjoy hearing themselves and their friends on tape. During the playback session, keep the critique of the soap opera on target. Concentrate on each group's successful interpretation of the script. Encourage the class to note effective pauses, emphases, inflections, instances of giving and taking, and successful development of two- or three-person scenes.

NINE Next, ask each team to play the recording of their best segment from the soap opera. Discuss the similarities or differences in the segment interpretations.

TEN The soap opera "Lexington Heights" activity presents three problems that the participants must solve with little or no supervision from the teacher:

- The group must produce a finished recording of the soap opera.

- The group recording must demonstrate an understanding of effective oral interpretation.

- Each group needs to learn to work collaboratively in a smooth and efficient manner. They are an ensemble.

Each group needs to learn to work collaboratively in a smooth and efficient manner. They are an ensemble.

ACTIVITY #3

Oral Interpretation

Purpose:

Actors learn how to prepare a piece for oral presentation and how to mark a script or text for oral interpretation.

EXERCISE A

Preparation:

ONE Before reading the poem "School Lunch" from Activity #3 in the *Student Handbook,* the entire class meets as one group. Have students take turns reading out loud the introductory material titled "Oral Interpretation."

TWO Then have students read orally the ten "Tips for Preparing an Oral Presentation" in the *Student Handbook.* You will continue reading aloud the section titled "Marking a Script for Oral Interpretation."

THREE Prior to this class meeting, you need to prepare a form for the section "Marking a Script for Oral Interpretation." Type a second nursery rhyme. Use the form on page 78 to reinforce script marking for this exercise.

Have students take turns reading out loud the introductory material titled "Oral Interpretation."

NAME: _____ DATE: _____

Oral Interpretation Form
Marking a Script for Oral Interpretation

Each participant is required to return this completed sheet to the instructor at the end of the activity.

1. Marking a script for word emphasis is a common form of notation. Underline the words or phrases which you feel should be read with greater strength or volume. Some actors feel that there is always one key word in every sentence. Even in a short sentence, it makes a difference which word gets emphasis.

2. Mark words that need to be spoken softly and with less volume. You can mark these words by putting them in parentheses.

3. Mark those words for which the sound of your voice goes up or down. The sound or pitch of your voice goes up when you ask a question. Show when your pitch goes up by drawing an arrow pointing upward. Draw an arrow pointing downward when you want to lower your pitch.

4. Show that a line or phrase should be spoken more quickly. Mark your script by drawing a bridge between words.

5. Remind yourself to slow down your reading. Put a slash between words.

6. If you want an actual pause, put two slashes between words.

In the space below, the instructor writes a second nursery rhyme. It will have no markings. As a class, students mark this rhyme for oral interpretation. Use this form to reinforce the exercise.

_____

_____

_____

_____

_____

_____

_____

_____

Execution:

ONE Before students read the poem "School Lunch" for Activity #3, the entire class meets as one group.

TWO Have students take turns reading out loud the introductory material titled "Oral Interpretation." Next, read orally the ten "Tips for Preparing an Oral Presentation" in the *Student Handbook*. During the discussion, stress that the students' first solo readings will be one to three minutes long. The audience will consist of fellow classmates.

THREE Continue reading aloud the section titled "Marking a Script for Oral Interpretation."

FOUR The instructor demonstrates "Marking a Script for Oral Interpretation" before the students begin working on their presentations. Give each student a copy of the nursery rhyme #2 focus sheet that you prepared prior to class. Have the entire group mark the rhyme for speaking. Have a volunteer present the piece to the class using the marking suggestions.

EXERCISE B

Purpose:

Actors practice their oral interpretation skills. Actors demonstrate meaning through voice and body movements.

Preparation:

ONE The first exercise, David Greenberg's poem "School Lunch," is a group project. The poem is located in the Appendix of the *Student Handbook*. The detailed explanation for Exercise B appears only in this *Teacher's Guide*.

Exercise B encourages participants to practice oral interpretation skills. They will demonstrate meaning through voice and body movements.

Several appropriate oral interpretation pieces are included in the Appendix of the *Student Handbook*. The *Teacher's Guide* suggests lesson plans for four oral interpretation selections. Instructors are encouraged to adapt all lessons throughout this text to best meet their needs and the needs of their students. Your students may enjoy performing all four selections or they may wish to present only two pieces.

Instructors are encouraged to adapt all lessons throughout this text to best meet their needs and the needs of their students.

Students often enjoy recording their oral interpretation work and listening to themselves and fellow classmates on tape.

TWO Students often enjoy recording their oral interpretation work and listening to themselves and fellow classmates on tape. If your students wish to record their sessions, you will need six to eight tape recorders for this lesson. Students may bring their own equipment. Gather all recording devices several days prior to Exercise B. In that way, there are few surprises and you will save time on the day of the exercise. Provide a locked cabinet or closet to store recorders safely overnight. Your school may be able to provide additional tape recorders.

THREE Prior to teaching this lesson, divide the class into groups of four to six students. Record the names of students in each group. Mix the experienced or confident actors with the shy or reluctant actors. Students build on each other's strengths.

FOUR If your students choose to record their sessions, prepare rehearsal recording stations around the room at the beginning of class. Preorganizing the stations saves class time and enables students to begin this activity quickly. Give each student the Oral Interpretation form on page 81 for marking a script for presentation.

FIVE Before this class meeting, prepare the form "Marking a Script for Oral Interpretation." Type lines at the bottom of the form. Have students write the poem "School Lunch" on every other line. In that way, they have room to make their oral interpretation markings.

NAME: _____ DATE: _____

Oral Interpretation Form
Marking a Script for Oral Interpretation

Each participant is required to return this completed sheet to the instructor at the end of the activity.

1. Marking a script for word emphasis is a common form of notation. <u>Underline the words or phrases</u> which you feel should be read with greater strength or volume. Some actors feel that there is always one key word in every sentence. Even in a short sentence, it makes a difference which word gets emphasis.

2. Mark words that need to be spoken softly and with less volume. You can mark these words by putting them in parentheses.

3. Mark those words in which the sound of your voice goes up or down. The sound or pitch of your voice goes up when you ask a question. Show when your pitch goes up by drawing an arrow pointing upward. Draw an arrow pointing downward when you want to lower your pitch.

4. Show that a line or phrase should be spoken more quickly. Mark your script by drawing a bridge between words.

5. Remind yourself to slow down your reading. Put a slash between words.

6. If you want an actual pause, put two slashes between words.

In the space below, students write the poem "School Lunch" on the lines and mark it for oral interpretation. Use this form for "Where Are the Words?", "Dog Days," and the rap, "Hey, I Can't Do That!"

_____

_____

_____

_____

_____

_____

_____

SIX In addition, give each student a focus form. Students complete the information on the focus sheet as they prepare their oral interpretation. Focus sheets make students accountable and enable participants to organize their groups promptly.

Focus forms provide a description of each person's job.

SEVEN Focus forms provide a description of each person's job. Moreover, focus forms keep students on task, give structure, organization, and purpose to the activity, and enable the instructor to know the role each team person played. A focus form for "School Lunch" follows on page 83. Each participant is required to return the completed focus sheet to the instructor at the close of Exercise A.

NAME: _____ DATE: _____

Oral Interpretation Focus Sheet

Procedure for rehearsing (name of piece) _____

The poems are located in the Appendix of the *Student Handbook.*

Each participant is required to return the completed focus sheet to the instructor at the end of the activity.

1. Choose a director. This person has the final authority regarding interpretation, assignment of parts for each student, and employing a group chorus. Everyone in the group chooses the director.

    The name of the director is: _____

2. If you are tape recording your session, choose one person to operate the recorder. If the group is small, the director and technical person may have speaking roles.

    The name of the technical person is: _____

3. Write the names of students and their spoken lines (parts) below.

    _____ reads lines _____

    _____ reads lines _____

    _____ reads lines _____

    _____ reads lines _____

4. Rehearse, tape, and play back. Give helpful comments. Change the way you read the poem. Then tape again. Which version is the best?

Version #1 _____ Version #2 _____

These are three reasons that Version # _____ is the best.

First, _____

_____

_____

Second, _____

_____

_____

Third, _____

_____

_____

EIGHT Some instructors like to separate the five or six groups into different rooms or areas. Other teachers like to keep the groups in one environment where they can see each group on task. You need to choose the method that best meets your needs and the needs of your students and principal.

NINE Again choose the location for the groups to assemble at the end of their group practice. The area can be the middle of the room. Planning and then explaining details to students ahead of time helps students succeed in all activities.

Remember: All procedures, forms, and comments are intended only as suggestions.

TEN Remember: All procedures, forms, and comments are intended only as suggestions. Every teacher brings specific strengths, experiences, and interests to class. Adapting a lesson to fit your needs makes the lesson more meaningful to you, the instructor.

EXERCISE B

School Lunch

Execution:

ONE Direct student attention to David Greenberg's poem "School Lunch." The poem is located in the Appendix of the *Student Handbook*.

TWO Give each student the sheet "Marking a Script for Oral Interpretation." Ask students to write the poem "School Lunch" on every other line at the bottom of the page. In that way, they have room to make their oral interpretation markings. The message of this poem is applicable to all school lunches, grades one through twelve. Whether students do individual interpretations or group presentations, students will enjoy this humorous piece.

THREE In addition, give each student a focus form. Students complete the information on the focus sheet as they prepare their oral interpretation. Focus sheets make students accountable and enable participants to organize their groups promptly.

FOUR Divide the class into five or six teams. Read the names of the students in each group. Assign each team a rehearsal station. If students wish to record their interpretations, provide a tape recorder for the team.

FIVE Create an imaginative interpretation of the poem "School Lunch." Two people can read a line together or another participant can read a line or section accompanied by a student chorus speaking or repeating words or lines. Students need to consider the following four points before rehearsing:

- The title and author must be announced. It is a part of the entire "reading."

- Students need to decide where and how individual group readers will stand.

- Will everyone remain "frozen"?

- Should some readers move before, during or after they have spoken?

SIX In order to create a successful oral interpretation, actors should read out loud, analyze, read out loud again, and then analyze the piece once more. Ultimately, actors will have a better understanding of the problems that an oral interpreter experiences and the techniques a performer can use to resolve them.

In order to create a successful oral interpretation, actors should read out loud, analyze, read out loud again, and then analyze the piece once more.

SEVEN Each group has twenty-five minutes to prepare a group reading of David Greenberg's poem. Every one on each team must participate. Some lines can be read solo while others are read in chorus. Oral interpretation brings literature to life. Therefore, it is important that each participant in the group understands the poem.

EIGHT The groups reconvene after twenty-five minutes. Since all of the groups have a diverse population, randomly choose two groups to present, or replay the recording of the best version of their oral interpretation piece, "School Lunch."

NINE After the performances, have each team identify those elements that created the best version of their reading of the poem. Concentrate on each group's successful interpretation of the script.

Encourage the entire class to note effective pauses, emphases, inflections, instances of giving and taking, and successful development of two- or three-person choral readings. Each group's interpretation is valid. Different interpretations often stress various aspects of a poem's meaning. Each interpretation helps the listeners understand the poem.

TEN INSTRUCTOR'S QUESTIONS FOR CLASS:

- How did each person or group create an effective interpretation of "School Lunch"?

- What feelings or ideas in the poem were best communicated?

- What was unclear or might have been improved in the readings?

ACTIVITY #4

Individual Performances

ONE Activity #4 does not appear in the *Student Handbook*. The explanation and detailed procedure for Exercises A, B, and C appear only in this text.

TWO Activity #4 introduces students to individual oral interpretations. It begins with Exercise A and Percy Leon Harris' poem "Where Are the Words?" All three poems selected for Activity #4 are located in the Appendix of the *Student Handbook*.

THREE For reluctant learners and shy students, it is possible for the team to present a group reading for each poem.

Your students may enjoy performing all three selections, or they may wish to present only one or two pieces.

FOUR Several additional appropriate oral interpretation pieces are included for your convenience in the Appendix of the *Student Handbook*. This *Teacher's Guide* suggests lesson plans for three of these selections. Instructors are encouraged to adapt all lessons throughout this text to best meet their needs and the needs of their students. Your students may enjoy performing all three selections, or they may wish to present only one or two pieces.

FIVE Students often enjoy recording their oral interpretation work and listening to themselves and fellow classmates on tape. If your students wish to record their sessions, you will need six to eight tape recorders for this lesson. Students may bring their own equipment.

SIX Gather all recording devices several days prior to this lesson. In that way, there are few surprises and you will save time on the day of the exercise. Provide a locked cabinet or closet to store recorders safely overnight. Perhaps your school can provide additional tape recorders.

SEVEN Prior to teaching this lesson, again divide your class into groups of four to six students. Record the names of students in each group. Again, mix experienced or confident actors with shy or reluctant actors. Attempt to create congenial diversity in each group.

Attempt to create congenial diversity in each group.

EIGHT If your students choose to record their sessions, prepare rehearsal recording stations around the room at the beginning of class. Preorganizing the stations saves class time and enables students to begin this activity quickly.

NINE Again, give each student a copy of the form "Marking a Script for Presentation." Students copy the poem "Where Are the Words?" on every other line at the bottom of the sheet. This format reinforces script marking before each of the oral interpretation recording sessions.

EXERCISE A

Where Are the Words?

INDIVIDUAL PERFORMANCES

Purpose:

Actors practice their oral interpretation skills. Actors demonstrate meaning through voice and body movements.

Execution:

ONE Give each student a copy of the sheet titled "Marking a Script for Oral Interpretation." Students copy the poem "Where Are the Words?" on every other line at the bottom of the page. This format reinforces script marking for oral interpretation.

TWO Direct student attention to the poem by Percy Leon Harris, "Where Are the Words?" The poem is located in the Appendix of the *Student Handbook*. Although Exercise A encourages individual performances, "Where Are the Words?" lends itself to group presentations.

THREE Demonstrate this exercise before the students begin their recording. Choose a volunteer to read the poem "Where Are the Words?" The second stanza is repeated at the end of the poem. Repeated phrases and stanzas often work well with group presentations. Ask students to offer constructive suggestions.

FOUR Everyone in the class is becoming more proficient with the process of preparing a piece for presentation. Have the demonstrator read the lines again, incorporating the students' suggestions. Explain to the class that the demonstrator is not expected to do a perfect job.

FIVE Divide the class into five or six teams. Read the names of the students in each group. Assign each team a rehearsal station. If students wish to record their interpretations, provide a tape recorder for the team. Students in each group prepare the same oral interpretation piece from the Appendix of the *Student Handbook*. The instructor may wish to substitute another suitable short piece.

SIX Students are encouraged to prepare an individual presentation. Each team should critique and help its members on their presentations. Students listen to each other and offer suggestions. Reluctant learners and shy students may prefer to present a group reading of "Where Are the Words?"

Each team should critique and help its members on their presentations.

In order to create a successful oral interpretation, actors should read out loud, analyze, read out loud again, and then analyze the piece once more. Ultimately, actors will have a fuller understanding of the problems that an oral interpreter experiences and the techniques a performer can use to resolve them.

SEVEN Each group has twenty-five minutes to prepare their individual or group reading of "Where Are the Words?" Everyone on a team must participate. Students can choose to read "Where Are the Words?" alone. Other students may choose to read the piece in pairs or as a group. Some lines can be read solo while others can be read in chorus. Oral interpretation brings literature to life. Therefore, it is important that each participant in the group understands the poem.

Students need to consider the following four points before rehearsing:

- The title and author must be announced. It is a part of the reading.

- Each student needs to decide where and how he/she will stand.

• Will the speaker remain in one place?

• Or should the reader move at appropriate times during the presentation?

EIGHT Then, when the teams reconvene, randomly choose one or two groups to present or play the tape of the best versions of each participant's interpretation of "Where Are the Words?"

NINE After the performances, have participants discuss those elements that created the best versions of their individual readings of the poem. Concentrate on each person's successful interpretation of the script. Encourage the entire class to note effective pauses, emphases, and inflections. Each person's interpretation is valid. Different interpretations often stress various aspects of a poem's meaning. All of the interpretations enable the listeners to understand the poem more fully.

> *Encourage the entire class to note effective pauses, emphases, and inflections. Each person's interpretation is valid.*

TEN INSTRUCTOR'S QUESTIONS FOR CLASS:

• How did each person or group create an effective interpretation of "Where Are the Words?"

• What feelings or ideas in the poem were best communicated?

• What was unclear or might have been improved in the readings?

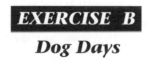

EXERCISE B
Dog Days

INDIVIDUAL PERFORMANCE

Purpose:

Actors practice their oral interpretation skills. Actors demonstrate meaning through voice and body movements.

Execution:

ONE Direct students' attention to Grace Glicken's poem "Dog Days." The piece is located in the Appendix of the *Student Handbook*.

Students are encouraged to prepare an individual presentation for "Dog Days." For reluctant learners and shy students, it is possible for the team to present a group reading of Glicken's "Dog Days."

Whether students do individual interpretations or group presentations, students will enjoy this poem. Each team should critique and help its members on their presentations. Encourage students to listen to each other and offer suggestions.

TWO Everyone in the class is now becoming more proficient with this process. Therefore, ask students to think of questions about the meaning of the poem.

THREE Use the same script marking sheet, "Marking a Script for Oral Interpretation," that you created for the previous two activities. On every other line at the bottom of the sheet, students copy the poem "Dog Days." This format reinforces script marking for oral interpretation.

FOUR Divide the class into five or six teams. Read the names of the students in each group. Assign each team a rehearsal station. If students wish to record their interpretations, provide tape recorders for the teams. Students in each group prepare the same oral interpretation piece from the Appendix of the *Student Handbook*. The instructor may wish to substitute another suitable short piece.

FIVE In order to create a successful oral interpretation, actors should read out loud, analyze, read out loud again, and then analyze the piece once more. Ultimately, actors will have a fuller understanding of the problems that an oral interpreter experiences and the techniques a performer can use to resolve them.

Oral interpretation brings literature to life. Therefore, it is important that each participant in the group understands the poem.

SIX Each group has twenty-five minutes to prepare their individual reading of "Dog Days." Everybody on the team prepares a reading. Oral interpretation brings literature to life. Therefore, it is important that each participant in the group understands the poem.

SEVEN The goal of each group: Each person will create an imaginative interpretation of the piece "Dog Days."

Students need to consider the following three points before rehearsing:

- The title and author must be announced. It is a part of the reading.

- Each student needs to decide where and how he/she will stand.

- Will the speaker remain in one place? Or should the reader move at appropriate times during the presentation?

EIGHT Then, when the teams reconvene, randomly choose one or two groups to present, or play the tape of, the best versions of each participant's interpretation of "Dog Days."

NINE After the performances, have each team discuss those elements that created the best version of their reading of Glicken's poem. Concentrate on each group's successful interpretation of the script. Encourage the entire class to note effective pauses, emphases, and inflections. Each person's interpretation is valid. Different interpretations often stress various aspects of this poem's meaning.

Different interpretations often stress various aspects of this poem's meaning.

TEN INSTRUCTOR'S QUESTIONS FOR CLASS:

- How did each person or group create an effective interpretation of "Dog Days"?

- What feelings or ideas in the poem were best communicated?

- What was unclear or might have been improved in the readings?

ELEVEN You may wish to choose your own selections for Activity #4. The short selections included in the Appendix of the *Student Handbook* are provided for the convenience of the instructor and the students. The pieces provide variety in genre and sophistication. Moreover, many of the choices contain some humor. However, the procedure outlined in this unit is more important than the suggested selections.

EXERCISE C

Hey! I Can't Do That!

INDIVIDUAL PERFORMANCE

Purpose:

Actors practice their oral interpretation skills. Actors demonstrate meaning through voice and body movements.

Execution:

ONE Direct students' attention to Ginny Weiss' rap poem, "Hey! I Can't Do That!" The selection is located in the Appendix of the *Student Handbook.*

Students are encouraged to prepare an individual presentation for "Hey! I Can't Do That!" For reluctant learners and shy students, it is possible for the team to present a group reading of "Hey! I Can't Do That!" This rap lends itself to movement and experimentation.

Whether students perform individual interpretations or group presentations, they will enjoy this fast-paced rap. All team members critique one another and help each other refine their presentations.

> *Whether students perform individual interpretations or group presentations, they will enjoy this fast-paced rap.*

TWO Everyone in the class is now becoming more proficient with this process. Therefore, ask students to think of questions about the meaning of the piece.

THREE Use the same script marking sheet, "Marking a Script for Oral Interpretation," that you created for the previous two activities. Students will write the poem "Hey! I Can't Do That!" on every other line at the bottom of the sheet. This format reinforces script marking for oral interpretation. The poem is located in the Appendix of the *Student Handbook.*

FOUR Divide the class into five or six teams. Read the names of the students in each group. Assign each team a rehearsal station. If students wish to record their interpretations, provide a tape recorder for the team. Students in each group prepare the same oral interpretation piece from the Appendix of the *Student Handbook.* The instructor may wish to substitute another suitable short piece.

FIVE In order to create a successful oral interpretation, actors should read out loud, analyze, read out loud again, and then analyze the piece once more. Ultimately, actors will have a fuller understanding of the problems that an oral interpreter experiences and the techniques a performer can use to resolve them. "Hey! I Can't Do That!" is lively. The poem encourages students to move as they rap. Tell students to experiment by emphasizing certain words and raising and lowering their voices.

SIX Each group has twenty-five minutes to prepare their individual or group reading of "Hey! I Can't Do That!" Everyone on each team must participate. Students can choose to read "Hey! I Can't Do That!" alone. Other students may choose to read the poem in pairs or as a group. Some lines can be read solo while others can be read in chorus. Oral interpretation brings literature to life. Therefore, it is important that each participant in the group understands the poem.

SEVEN The goal of each group: Each person will create an imaginative interpretation of the piece "Hey! I Can't Do That!"

Students need to consider the following three points before rehearsing:

- The title and author must be announced. It is a part of the reading.

- Each student needs to decide where and how he/she will stand.

- Will the speaker remain in one place? Or should the reader move at appropriate times during the presentation?

EIGHT Then, when the teams reconvene, randomly choose one or two groups to present, or play the tape, of the best versions of each participant's interpretation of "Hey! I Can't Do That!"

NINE After the performances, have each team discuss those elements that created the best version of their reading of the poem. Concentrate on each group's successful interpretation of the script. Encourage the entire class to note effective pauses, emphases, and inflections. Each person's interpreta-

Ultimately, actors will have a fuller understanding of the problems that an oral interpreter experiences and the techniques a performer can use to resolve them.

tion is valid. Different interpretations often stress various aspects of a poem's meaning.

TEN INSTRUCTOR'S QUESTIONS FOR CLASS:

- How did each person or group create an effective interpretation of "Hey! I Can't Do That!"?

- What feelings or ideas in the poem were best communicated?

- What was unclear or might have been improved in the readings?

ELEVEN You may wish to choose your own selections for Activity #4. The short selections included in the Appendix of the *Student Handbook* are provided for the convenience of the instructor and the students. The pieces provide variety in genre and sophistication. Many of the choices contain some humor. The procedure outlined in this unit is more important than the suggested selections.

The procedure outlined in this unit is more important than the suggested selections.

Activity #4's objective is to provide everyone in the class a positive, successful experience in oral interpretation. Everyone can experience a sense of accomplishment with this activity.

NOTE

TALENT DAY

This unit gave students the opportunity to make choices. Unit activities gave students the chance to perform. In theatre, an actor needs to practice his craft constantly. He needs to perform many times. Talent Day gives the students experience in performing before an audience. Participants have a chance to shine! Following are several choices for Talent Day.

1. Find a poem, monolog, or short passage that they like. Present it as an oral interpretation reading.

2. Find a short or funny sketch. Recruit class members to play the parts. Rehearse the scene. Memorize the lines. Present it in front of the class.

3. Choose one of the radio commercials on which they worked. Revise it. Make it into a television commercial. Perform it before the class. If equipment is available, students can videotape the commercial. Then actors can play the tape for the class.

4. Write a short play or another episode of the soap opera, "Lexington Heights." With the aid of some classmates, present a reading of the scene or play.

UNIT SUMMARY

Unit Three stressed a variety of skills and theatre values. Write the following short list of theatre values on the board. Reading and discussing the list reinforces the behaviors.

Theatre education stresses that: (1) participants need to work hard if they want to succeed; (2) participants need to practice their new skills in order to be proficient; (3) participants need to aim high in their goals; (4) participants need to strive for excellence in all of their work; and (5) participants need to work cooperatively with a group.

...participants need to work hard if they want to succeed...

Following is a list of five skills participants learned in this unit:

1. Gained experience in oral expression by rehearsing and recording a radio commercial.

[Participants] gained skill and experience in preparing short literary pieces for oral interpretation.

2. Gained skill and experience preparing and tape recording a soap opera script.

3. Gained skill and experience in preparing short literary pieces for oral interpretation.

4. Learned ten tips for preparing any piece for presentation.

5. Learned how to mark a script or text for oral interpretation.

UNIT FOUR
Necessary and Interpretive Actions

Unit Four concentrates on the mechanics of moving gracefully on a proscenium stage. The philosophy of the *Student Handbook* is that students learn by doing. There is no attempt to provide a definitive list of dos and don'ts for students to memorize. Instead, the *Teacher's Guide* provides exercises that enable students to discover the basic rules for necessary and interpretive actions. The *Student Handbook* clearly defines the purpose of each activity. In addition, specific directions and procedural steps are included for each exercise in the *Student Handbook*.

Unit Four concentrates on the mechanics of moving gracefully on a proscenium stage. The philosophy of the Student Handbook is that students learn by doing.

In this unit students develop four basic skills.

- Participants learn to identify necessary actions in a script.

- Participants develop interpretive actions using shadow scenes.

- Participants learn to make sense out of nonsense through movement.

- Participants develop an understanding of stage pictures.

Unit Four applies the same classroom management techniques as Unit Three — divide and conquer. Working in small groups, students benefit in four ways.

- Participants share responsibilities working with and encouraging other group members.

- Participants share the process of discovering solutions to acting problems.

- Participants share their created scenes with the entire group.

- Participants experience more individual attention.

Two weekly calendars summarizing each day's activities follow. Calendars are provided for your convenience so that you can quickly review each week's activities ahead of time or give a copy of your weekly syllabus to your principal or department chairperson.

UNIT FOUR: NECESSARY AND INTERPRETIVE ACTIONS

MONDAY	TUESDAY	WEDNESDAY	THURSDAY	FRIDAY
DAY ONE *ACTIVITY #1* (1) Class members read aloud the opening two pages of Unit Four. (2) Two students demonstrate "Necessary Actions" in the short Sue-Richard scene. (3) Do Activity #1. Read directions aloud. (4) Commentary for the five short scenes is written in the *Teacher's Guide*. (5) If time, have students read aloud introductory material for "Interpretive Actions" in the *Student Handbook*.	*DAY TWO* *ACTIVITY #2* (1) Students reread script fragments. Students focus on "Recognizing Interpretive Actions." (2) Students read aloud introductory paragraphs of "Shadow Scenes." Students read directions for "Shadow Scenes" and information following five scenes. (3) Begin Activity #2. Assign "Shadow Scene" parts to two students. They choose a *who*, a *where*, and a *what*. (4) Divide class into groups. Do the assignment explained in the Lesson Plan.	*DAY THREE* *ACTIVITY #3* (1) Each small group creates five interpretations of a shadow scene. (2) After groups complete activity, each group performs for class. (3) Audience members identify the *who, where,* and *what* of each scene. (4) If time, have class read aloud "Nonsense Dialog," Activity #3. Read the page of commentary following. (5) Begin Activity #3. Select any four students. Assign six lines of nonsense dialog. Actors read six lines.	*DAY FOUR* *ACTIVITY #4* (1) Explain "Sample Nonsense Solution." Actors recreate sensible scene from nonsense lines. (2) Divide class into groups of four. (3) Activity #3 — Students create sensible scene from same six lines. (4) Write four additional settings for the six lines of dialog on board. (5) Students reconvene after completion of exercise. (6) Students identify the *who, where,* and *what* of each team's scene.	*DAY FIVE* *ACTIVITY #5* *EXERCISE A* (1) Activity #4 — Class reads aloud section titled "Stage Pictures." (2) Choose any two actors to read parts in "Shadow Scene A." Actors silently stage single frozen picture. Audience identifies the *who, where,* and *what* of "Shadow Scene A." (3) Choose two other actors to read parts in "Shadow Scene B." Actors silently stage single frozen picture. Audience identifies the *who, where,* and *what* of "Shadow Scene B."

WEEK AT A GLANCE: WEEK ONE

UNIT FOUR: NECESSARY AND INTERPRETIVE ACTIONS

MONDAY	TUESDAY	WEDNESDAY	THURSDAY	FRIDAY
DAY SIX *ACTIVITY #5* *EXERCISE B* (1) Activity #5 — Direct students attention to short script "The Mortgage." Ask three actors to read script. 2) Then have students read aloud directions for Activity #5 — Part B. (3) Divide class into groups of six. Three actors on each team create stage picture for "The Mortgage." The second trio creates its version of same scene. Each trio arranges characters in a dramatic pose. (4) Reconvene at completion of exercise. Actors demonstrate stage pictures.	*DAY SEVEN* *ACTIVITY #6* *EXERCISE C* (1) Direct class's attention to Activity #6 — Part C. The script "The Mortgage" continues. Read the new script section aloud. (2) Then have students read aloud directions for Activity #6 — Part C. (3) Divide class into groups of five. Scene now has four actors. The fifth person is group's director. (4) Each group creates stage picture for new scene in "The Mortgage." (5) Evaluation when groups reconvene.	*DAY EIGHT* *ACTIVITY #7* *EXERCISE D* (1) Direct class's attention to Activity #7 — Part D. Review seven questions to ask before preparing "Tableaux." (2) Divide class into groups of seven. (3) Each group tells story of Adam and Eve in five tableaux. Each team has six actors and one director. (4) Give groups different directions. Allow ten minutes to prepare tableaux. (5) Reconvene. Students identify the *who, where,* and *what* of each tableau.	*DAY NINE* *UNIT SUMMARY* (1) Use this day to complete Activity #7 — Part D if class has not finished the exercise. (2) Have students read aloud the Unit Summary at end of Unit Four. (3) Next, ask a student to read aloud the skills learned in Unit Four. Students benefit from reviewing the skills they have learned.	

WEEK AT A GLANCE: WEEK TWO

ACTIVITY #1

Recognizing Necessary Actions

Purpose:

Students learn to recognize and demonstrate necessary actions in a script.

Preparation:

ONE The term, *necessary action,* refers to the relationship between words in a script and movement on a stage. Sometimes written stage directions state specifically how actors should move. For example, an author might write the following direction: *(They sit down.).* That is a necessary action and the actors should sit. Other necessary actions can be required by specific words in the dialog. Direct students' attention to Sue-Richard dialog.

TWO Preview the first two pages of Unit Four in the *Student Handbook.* Plan to discuss the term *necessary actions.*

THREE DEMONSTRATION: On the day that you introduce Activity #1, have two students demonstrate necessary actions in the simple scene between Sue and Richard found in the *Student Handbook.*

Execution:

ONE The *necessary actions* for each of the five script fragments in the *Student Handbook* are written in *italics* on the following page. Additional comments are noted afterwards in regular print.

TWO Direct students' attention to the first two pages of Unit Four in the *Student Handbook.* Have students read the introductory material out loud. Discuss the term *necessary actions.*

THREE Have two students demonstrate necessary actions in the simple scene between Sue and Richard.

FOUR Next, have students read the directions for Activity #1. Students complete Activity #1.

FIVE Commentary on the necessary actions for each of the five short scenes follows.

Scene 1. One necessary action: *Lois takes a knife from the drawer.* Stage directions are to be interpreted

> *The term, **necessary action,** refers to the relationship between words in a script and movement on a stage.*

as necessary actions. In actuality, directors or actors sometimes disregard stage directions or change them. However, an author writes them with the expectation that the actor will follow them.

Scene 2. Two necessary actions: 1) *Roger takes a step toward Jane.* 2) *Jane screams at the top of her voice.* Vocal inflection is included as an "action." When you discuss interpretive actions repeat this point.

Scene 3. Two necessary actions: 1) *The inspector picks up the telephone receiver,* and, most likely, 2) *he jiggles the button or cradle which normally activates the phone.*

Scene 4. Three necessary actions: 1) *Marvin talks breathlessly.* 2) *Marvin collapses to the ground.* 3) *George sees Marvin on the ground.*

Scene 5. One necessary action: *Norman is dealing cards.*

ACTIVITY #2

Recognizing Interpretive Actions

Purpose:

Students learn to choose appropriate interpretive actions.

Preparation:

> *Interpretive actions are actions that are not necessary in the script. If the action is omitted, the actor's words will still make sense.*

ONE *Interpretive actions* refer to the relationship between words in a script and movement on a stage. Movements that are not written specifically by the author are called interpretive actions. Interpretive actions are actions that are not necessary in the script. If the action is omitted, the actor's words will still make sense.

TWO Plan to have students read out loud the introductory material for "Interpretive Actions" in Unit Four of the *Student Handbook.* Discuss the term **INTERPRETIVE ACTIONS.**

THREE On the day that you introduce "Recognizing Interpretive Actions," ask two students to demonstrate interpretive actions in the previous five short scenes.

Execution:

ONE Direct student attention to Unit Four in the *Student Handbook*. Have students read out loud the introductory material for interpretive actions. Discuss the term *interpretative actions*.

TWO Students reread each of the five script fragments from Activity #1. During the rereading, students now concentrate on interpretive actions. Interpretive actions mean that the actor chooses appropriate, reasonable movements. Stress that they should be logical and make sense.

THREE Examples of interpretive actions from the five script fragments from Activity #1 are noted below.

> *Interpretive actions mean that the actor chooses appropriate, reasonable movements.*

Scene 1. Two interpretive actions: 1) *Bill puts his hands on his hips.* 2) *Lois smiles sardonically.*

Scene 2. Three interpretive actions: 1) *Jane retreats behind a car.* 2) *Roger pops a mint in his mouth, pauses, and then* 3) *speaks in a menacing voice.*

Scene 3. Three interpretive actions: 1) *The inspector puffs slowly on his pipe* 2) *as he gazes at the murder victim.* 3) *Then he strolls briskly over to the telephone table.*

Scene 4. Two interpretive actions: 1) *Marvin puts his hand faintly to his forehead.* 2) *George rushes over to Marvin and kneels beside him.*

Scene 5. Three interpretive actions: 1) *Norman makes a flicking sound* 2) *as he turns over each card.* 3) *He looks at Sally over the top of his glasses.*

FOUR Then, have students read out loud in the *Student Handbook* the introductory material for "Shadow Scenes."

FIVE Third, have students read the directions, the "Shadow Scenes," and the information following the shadow scenes.

ACTIVITY #3

Developing Interpretive Actions for "Shadow Scenes"

Purpose:

Students develop several different interpretive actions using a shadow scene.

Preparation:

ONE The "Shadow Scenes" are written as an acting exercise. They have no stage directions. The dialog contains intentionally vague words. When working with shadow scenes, actors decide on the *who, where,* and *what* of the scene. They try to create as many interpretations as possible. Actors give meaning to unclear dialog through the use of interpretive actions.

> **When working with shadow scenes, actors decide on the who, where, *and* what of the scene.**

TWO Before this activity, divide your class into groups of four. Record the names of students in each group. Attempt to mix experienced or confident actors with shy or reluctant actors. Students build on each other's strengths.

THREE Create a list of assigned parts for each group. The day before this lesson, tell each student his/her part. Encourage students to memorize their lines before Activity #3 begins. Alert participants that they have one day to memorize their short parts. You may wish to allow students in each group to choose their own parts.

FOUR Finding appropriate interpretive actions is the main focus of the activity. The activity moves quickly, easily, and successfully when students memorize their lines. Participants experience a sense of competence and pride when they memorize their lines.

FIVE On the day that you introduce "Developing Interpretive Actions," plan to ask two students to read the script "Shadow Scene A."

SIX On the day of the activity, some instructors like to separate their groups into different rooms or areas. Other teachers like to keep the groups in one environment where they can see each group on task. Again, you choose the best method to meet your needs and the needs of your students and principal.

SEVEN Choose the location where you wish all five or six groups to meet at the completion of their rehearsal sessions. The area can be as simple as the middle of the room. Planning details ahead of time helps students succeed in this activity.

Execution:

ONE Assign the parts for "Shadow Scene A" to two students. In front of the class, the two actors decide on a *who*, a *where*, and a *what*. Then they read the script "Shadow Scene A" from Unit Four in the *Student Handbook.*

TWO As you have done in previous lessons, divide the class into five or six teams. Read the names of the students in each section. Assign "Shadow Scene A" to two teams. Next, assign "Shadow Scene B" to two other teams. Lastly, assign "Alternate Version: Shadow Scene B" to the remaining two groups.

THREE ASSIGNMENT: Students in each group develop five creative interpretations of their assigned shadow scene. Each student needs to memorize his/her short part for the scene to be successful. The activity moves quickly and easily when students memorize their lines. Finding appropriate interpretive actions is the main focus of this activity. Allow ten to fifteen minutes for students to prepare and rehearse their five shadow scenes.

FOUR After the groups have completed the exercise, they return to the designated meeting place. Each team performs its two favorite shadow scene interpretations. Next, participants discuss their choice of interpretive actions. Audience members identify the *who, where,* and *what* of each scene and note effective pauses, actions, and inflections.

> *Audience members identify the* **who, where,** *and* **what** *of each scene and note effective pauses, actions, and inflections.*

ACTIVITY #4

Nonsense Dialog

Purpose:

Students learn to create meaning through movement and actions on stage.

Preparation:

ONE Familiarize yourself with Activity #4, "Nonsense Dialog," in Unit Four of the *Student Handbook*. Read the six lines of nonsense dialog and the commentary. In addition, closely review the following suggested blocking solution.

TWO The following sample solution appears only in this *Teacher's Guide.*

Practicing nonsense dialog forces students to make their movement meaningful.

Sample Nonsense Solution
Four Actors in Scene

(The setting is the corner drugstore. Three ten-year-old children are huddled around the greeting card rack, reading the messages in the cards and giggling. The proprietor is nearby rearranging some merchandise on a shelf. He/she has a problem with children loitering in the store and shoplifting.)

CHILD #1: *(Choosing a card, giggling, and then reading it aloud in an overly dramatic voice to his/her companions)* The stars shine like torches in the night. *(The children giggle.)*

CHILD #2: *(Finding a card that makes no sense to him/her whatsoever and reading it like a question)* Tony pulled the fire alarm and ran? *(Again, the three look at the picture and caption on the card and giggle.)*

(The proprietor, who is annoyed, walks over to the three children, scowls and clears his throat. The children appear unphased. They have been through this routine before.)

CHILD #1: *(Showing dollar bill and asking sheepishly)* May I have some baby powder, please?

(The proprietor takes the dollar bill brusquely and disappears. The children go back to selecting strange or amusing cards.)

CHILD #3: *(Reading)* Why doesn't anyone care about baby seals? *(They giggle.)*

CHILD #2: *(Reading)* Sometimes I don't understand you. *(They giggle.)*

(The proprietor returns with baby powder and change in hand, thrusts it at Child #1, and scowls at the three.)

PROPRIETOR: *(Pointing to the door)* I want you out of here by the time I count to ten!

THREE ADDITIONAL SETTINGS FOR THE NONSENSE DIALOG: After the demonstration in Activity #4, suggest these settings for the nonsense dialog in the *Student Handbook*.

- A classroom. The teacher is lecturing and writing on the board. Some students are whispering and passing notes.

- A large party.

- A mental hospital.

- A room with a television turned on.

FOUR Prior to Activity #4, divide your class into groups of four to six students. Some students may have to speak two lines. As in past exercises, mix experienced or confident actors with shy or reluctant actors. Record the names of students in each group.

FIVE On the day of this activity, tell students to quickly memorize their short parts in class. The activity moves quickly, easily, and successfully when students memorize their lines. Participants experience a sense of competence and pride in their group's accomplishment when they memorize their lines.

SIX To introduce Activity #4, "Making Sense Out of Nonsense Through Movement," ask four students to read the six lines of the nonsense dialog printed in the *Student Handbook.*

SEVEN On a first reading, the participants do not attempt to make sense out of nonsense through movement in this demonstration. On a second reading, you will suggest the setting from the sample nonsense solution detailed above. Actors then create a sensible scene from the nonsense dialog. Students realize that they can make sense from dialog in any scene if they understand the *who, where,* and *what* of that scene.

EIGHT On the day of the activity, some instructors like to separate their groups into different rooms or areas. Other teachers like to keep the groups in one environment where they can see each group on task. Again, you choose the best method to meet your needs and the needs of your students and principal.

NINE Choose the location where you wish all five or six groups to meet at the completion of their rehearsal sessions. The area can be as simple as the middle of the room. Planning details ahead of time helps students succeed in this activity.

Execution:

ONE BRIEF DEMONSTRATION #1: Randomly select four students. Assign the six lines of the nonsense dialog printed in the *Student Handbook.* In front of the class, each volunteer merely reads one or two sentences in the nonsense script beginning, "The stars shine like torches in the night..." During

Participants experience a sense of competence and pride in their group's accomplishment when they memorize their lines.

this first reading, participants do not attempt to make sense out of nonsense through movement.

TWO BRIEF DEMONSTRATION #2: Describe the "Sample Nonsense Dialog Solution" to the demonstrators. Then ask the four actors to create the drugstore scene. Each actor says his line from the nonsense dialog. Offer simple direction for the actors. Actors then create a sensible scene from the nonsense dialog. Students realize that they can make sense from dialog in any scene if they understand the *who, where,* and *what* of that scene.

THREE Now, divide the class into groups of four to six actors. Read the names of the students in each section. All groups will work with the same six lines of dialog.

FOUR Students create a sensible scene out of the same six lines of nonsense dialog. Each student quickly needs to memorize his/her short part for the scene to be successful.

FIVE ADDITIONAL SETTINGS FOR THE NONSENSE DIALOG: After the demonstration in Activity #4, suggest these settings for the nonsense dialog in the *Student Handbook*.

- A classroom. The teacher is lecturing and writing on the board. Some students are whispering and passing notes.

- A large party.

- A mental hospital.

- A room with a television turned on.

Allow ten to fifteen minutes for students to block and prepare their nonsense dialog so that it is logical and makes sense to others.

SIX After the groups have completed the exercise, they return to the designated meeting place. Each team performs its scene. Next, participants discuss their choice of interpretive actions.

SEVEN EVALUATION: Audience members identify the *who, where,* and *what* of each scene. Students note effective pauses, actions, and inflections. In summary, stress that each group showed how words alone can sometimes be confusing. However, those same words coupled with actions can amuse, inform, or clarify.

> *Students realize that they can make sense from dialog in any scene if they understand the who, where, and what of that scene.*

ACTIVITY #5

Stage Pictures

Purpose:

Students learn to recognize pivotal scenes in the plot of a play.

Preparation:

ONE Stage pictures are like snapshots of climactic moments. They exist in every scene of a play. A good stage picture suggests the dramatic conflict that has been building in a given scene.

TWO Remind students that a director considers the following four ideas when composing a stage picture:

- Where characters will be standing at the climactic moment.

- How close they will be to one another.

- Who will be looking at whom.

- And which character(s) will have the central focus.

THREE On the day that you introduce stage pictures be prepared to ask two students to reread "Shadow Scene A." During this reading, volunteers silently stage a single frozen picture for Scene A. Ask students to recall the *who, where,* and *what* for this "Shadow Scene A" stage picture.

FOUR Choose two additional students to reread "Shadow Scene B." During this reading, volunteers silently stage a single frozen picture for Scene B. Ask students to recall the *who, where,* and *what* for this "Shadow Scene B" stage picture.

FIVE For Exercise B, you want to divide your class into groups of six. As in past exercises, try to mix experienced or confident actors with shy or reluctant actors. Students build on each other's strengths.

Take time to record the names of students in each group. In Exercise B, "The Mortgage," the short scene has three characters. Therefore, you will need two sets of three performers.

SIX Several days prior to Exercise B, create a list of assigned parts for each trio of students in the designated groups. In class tell each student his part. You may wish to allow the actors in

> *Stage pictures are like snapshots of climactic moments. They exist in every scene of a play.*

> *Students need to understand their parts in order to compose a successful stage picture.*

each trio to select their own parts. Students need to understand their parts in order to compose a successful stage picture.

SEVEN For Exercise C, divide your class into groups of five. Then list the names of students in each group. In Exercise C, "The Mortgage," the new short scene has four characters. One person will serve as the director and arrange the actors in a dramatic pose. Use the procedure described above for assigning parts for Exercise C, "The Mortgage." Students need to understand their parts in order to compose another successful stage picture.

EIGHT On the day of the activity, some instructors like to separate their groups into different rooms or areas. Other teachers like to keep the groups in one environment where they can see each group on task. Again, you choose the best method to meet your needs and the needs of your students and principal.

NINE Choose the location where you wish all five or six groups to meet at the completion of both and activities. The area can be as simple as the middle of the room. Planning details ahead of time helps students succeed in this activity.

EXERCISE A

Purpose:

Students demonstrate an understanding of stage pictures through their portrayal of frozen pictures for "Shadow Scenes A" and "B."

Execution:

ONE Direct students' attention to the section titled "Stage Pictures" in Unit Four in the *Student Handbook*. Have students read the introductory material out loud.

TWO At random, choose two students to read the parts in "Shadow Scene A." During this reading, volunteers silently stage a single frozen picture for Scene A. Ask students to recall the *who, where,* and *what* from this "Shadow Scene A" stage picture.

THREE Choose two additional students to read the parts in "Shadow Scene B." During this reading, volunteers silently stage a single frozen picture for Scene B. Ask students to recall the *who, where,* and *what* from this "Shadow Scene B" stage picture.

Exercise B

Purpose:

Students create a single stage picture for "The Mortgage."

Execution:

ONE Direct students' attention to the section titled Exercise B in Unit Four in the *Student Handbook*. Ask three students to read the short script, "The Mortgage," out loud.

TWO Students read out loud the directions for Exercise B. Next, ask students to read the explanation that follows in the text. Students will have a better understanding of the activity if they read about the exercise first.

THREE Divide the class into groups of six. On each team, three students will create a stage picture for "The Mortgage." The second trio of actors will create their own version of the same scene. Each trio arranges the three characters in a dramatic pose.

FOUR Imagine that this pose will be used as a publicity photograph for the newspaper. Slight changes in emphasis will alter the nature of conflict. Most likely, each team will stage a distinct tableau because they will emphasize different aspects of the short scene. Allow ten minutes for students to prepare their stage pictures.

FIVE After the groups have completed the exercise, participants return to the designated meeting place. Each team demonstrates its stage picture. Next, participants discuss their choice of interpretive actions. Audience members identify the exact line each stage picture highlights.

> *Students will have a better understanding of the activity if they read about the exercise first.*

Exercise C

Purpose:

Students create a single stage picture for "The Mortgage."

Execution:

ONE Direct student attention to the section titled Exercise C in Unit Four in the *Student Handbook*. The short script "The Mortgage" continues. Ask four students to read out loud the new script segment.

TWO Next, have students read aloud the directions for Exercise C. Then students read the explanation that follows in the text. Students will have a better understanding of the activity if they read it first.

THREE Divide the class into groups of five. Remind students that the scene now has four people. The fifth person will serve as the director. Ask if the focus has changed.

FOUR On each team, four actors will create a stage picture for "The Mortgage." The group's student director arranges the four characters in a dramatic pose. Actors also are encouraged to contribute to the staging process.

FIVE Most likely, each team will stage a distinct tableau that will emphasize different aspects of the short scene. Imagine that this pose will be used as a publicity photograph for the newspaper. Allow ten minutes for students to prepare their stage pictures.

SIX After the groups have completed the exercise, they return to the designated meeting place. Each team demonstrates its stage picture. Audience members identify the exact line each stage picture highlights.

EXERCISE D

Purpose:

Students tell a familiar tale in a series of five stage pictures.

Preparation:

> **A tableau is a still picture that tells a story without words. Still pictures exist in scenes of a play.**

ONE A tableau is a still picture that tells a story without words. Still pictures exist in scenes of a play. A good stage picture suggests the dramatic conflict that has been building in a given scene.

TWO Review the seven questions in the *Student Handbook* following the directions for Exercise D.

THREE Actors need to decide which character is the most important in the still picture. Which scene will be the first in the five tableaux?

FOUR Prior to Activity #5, divide the class into groups of seven. List the names of students in each group. Attempt to mix experienced or confident actors with shy or reluctant actors. Students build on each other's strengths. Create two or three equally balanced groups. Strive to have the same ratio of males and females in each group.

FIVE Plan to allow five to ten minutes for students to prepare their tableaux.

Execution:

ONE Direct student attention to section titled Exercise D in Unit Four in the *Student Handbook*. Next, before dividing the class into sections, ask students to read out loud the directions for Exercise D.

TWO Review the seven questions students need to consider when they prepare their tableaux. Students will have a better understanding of the activity if they know what is expected of them.

THREE Divide the class into groups of seven.

FOUR Each group will tell the story of Adam and Eve in the Garden of Eden in five tableaux. There are six character parts:

- Adam

- Eve

- Serpent

- God

- Tree of Knowledge

- Animals in the Garden of Eden

Each group does not have to use all six characters in their tableaux. Groups can highlight two to six characters in one tableau. The seventh person on each team is the director whose role is to interpret the scenes.

FIVE Give each group different directions. Tell group #1 that Adam is the central and most important character. Tell group #2 that Eve is the most important character. Tell the story from Eve's point of view. Tell group #3 that the serpent is the most important character in their five tableaux. Tell group #4 that God is the central character. Tell the story from God's point of view. Tell group #5 nothing. Only tell them that the scenes should be from the point of view of only one of the six characters.

> *Students will have a better understanding of the activity if they know what is expected of them.*

SIX Allow each group to use one chair on which to stand or sit if they wish. All other props, such as an apple, are represented by a frozen pantomime.

SEVEN Students have five to ten minutes to prepare their tableaux.

EIGHT After the groups have completed the exercise, they return to the designated meeting place. Each team performs all five scenes from their tableaux. Audience members identify the *who, where,* and *what* of the tableaux. Follow the procedure for presenting tableaux outlined in Exercise D in the *Student Handbook*.

Each group chooses an audience member to tell the story represented by the group's five still pictures. If the audience member tells the story successfully from the tableaux, then the actors and the director know they have been successful.

> *If the audience member tells the story successfully from the tableaux, then the actors and the director know they have been successful.*

NINE DISCUSSION QUESTIONS:

- Did the scenes vary from group to group?

- How can they be different? Aren't the groups all preparing the same familiar story?

- What could possibly make the groups' tableaux different? Actually, each group was not preparing the exact same story. Why? Because each team was telling the Bible story from a different character's point of view.

- Is there one scene among all that we have seen today that is more effective?

- Why is this scene more effective?

- What particular interpretations did the director choose?

- Did the director pose the actors in a specific dynamic manner? How?

TEN This is a good time to discuss directing and a director's concept of a particular play. There is a difference between interpretation and copyright infringement. When authors write plays, they do not want actors or directors to change their words or sentences. In fact, it is against copyright law to delete dialog from a play performance without specific permission from the author.

However, authors understand that each director may interpret a line or a scene differently. One director might sense that a play has a political message. Other directors may view the play they are staging as a metaphor. Still other directors look for a key phrase or speech within a play which captures the essence of the play.

Ultimately, though, most directors have a distinct point of view. Their point of view influences the decisions they make arranging characters on stage and instructing the actors how to move and deliver their lines. Ideally, actors understand and share the directorial concept. Everyone works together to give that concept stronger focus in the production. This need for focus exists in comedy as well as drama. A writer understands that directors may interpret a play differently than the writer intended.

Ideally, actors understand and share the directorial concept. Everyone works together to give that concept stronger focus in the production.

UNIT SUMMARY

In Unit Four, participants learned how stage movement adds meaning to the words actors speak in a play. Five activities helped students discover various ways an actor can express a character's thoughts with gestures, body language, facial expressions, and eye contact.

Following is a list of five skills participants learned in this unit:

1. Learned to recognize **necessary actions.**

2. Learned to develop **interpretive actions.**

3. Learned to create sense out of nonsense through movement.

4. Learned to understand characters' motives through still stage pictures.

5. Learned to cooperate with other actors and a director in the process of creating scenes.

UNIT FIVE
Blocking a Scene

Unit Four concentrated on the mechanics of moving gracefully on a proscenium stage. Unit Five emphasizes the special vocabulary that theatre people use in describing that movement. Theatre has created its own language. In all languages, comprehension and communication evolve from an understanding of words. Students need to learn the theatre vocabulary in order to be successful on stage. Unit Five contains a unit test that teachers can use to assess student comprehension of the terms.

In all languages, comprehension and communication evolve from an understanding of words.

The *Student Handbook* clearly defines the purpose of each activity. Moreover, specific directions and procedural steps are included for each exercise in the *Student Handbook*. In this unit students develop four basic skills:

- Participants learn stage terms necessary for blocking a scene.

- Participants learn to demonstrate a character's dominance through blocking.

- Participants learn memorizing techniques.

- Participants rehearse and perform a short segment of a one-act play.

Unit Five applies the same classroom management techniques as Unit Four. Working in small groups, students benefit by:

- Sharing responsibilities with other group members,

- Sharing the process of discovering solutions to acting problems, and

- Sharing their created scenes with the entire group.

Two weekly calendars summarizing daily lessons follow. The calendar format is provided for your convenience so that you can quickly review each week's activities ahead of time or give a copy of your weekly syllabus to your principal or department chairperson.

UNIT FIVE: BLOCKING A SCENE

MONDAY	TUESDAY	WEDNESDAY	THURSDAY	FRIDAY
DAY ONE *ACTIVITY #1* *EXERCISE A*	*DAY TWO* *ACTIVITY #2*	*DAY THREE* *ACTIVITY #3*	*DAY FOUR* *GETTING READY*	*DAY FIVE*
(1) Activity #1, Exercise A — "Stage Terms and an Actor's Body Positions." Mark the stage with stage diagram from Unit Five. (2) Select three students. Have students stand on-stage. (3) Call stage directions to students. Volunteers will stand in appropriate places. (4) "Actor's Body Positions" — Select three new volunteers. Follow demonstration script in *Teacher's Guide*. Students respond with proper body positions.	(1) Activity #2 — Blocking "A Family Difference." Students read aloud introductory material on blocking. (2) Ask two students to read "A Family Difference." (3) Students continue reading aloud, "Blocking a Scene." (4) Read aloud directions for Activities #2 and #3. (5) Assign parts to two students who perform the script, "A Family Difference." (6) Groups block scene. Parent is dominant character.	(1) Activity #3 — Students remain in same groups. Same pairs within group re-block "A Family Difference." (2) Change blocking to make child dominant. (3) View members of group and make suggestions. (4) Students gather at a central meeting place. (5) Pairs demonstrate blocking for Activity #2. (6) Viewers identify effective blocking choices.	(1) Assign parts to students now for pre-blocked scene segments in Activity #3. (2) Do Exercise A, "Memorizing Dialog." Students read out loud nine tips for memorizing dialog. (3) Do Exercise B, "Getting Ready for Activity #3." Students read out loud "Acting a Pre-blocked Scene." (4) Class reads aloud "Directions." (5) Read synopses for three scenes. See instructions in the *Teacher's Guide*.	(1) Begin Activity #5. Divide class into groups of six. (2) Each team reads aloud their assigned scene segment. (3) Each team marks scene's group plan on rehearsal area floor. (4) Pairs begin to interpret pre-blocking notations.

WEEK AT A GLANCE: WEEK ONE

UNIT FIVE: BLOCKING A SCENE

MONDAY	TUESDAY	WEDNESDAY	THURSDAY	FRIDAY
DAY SIX *ACTIVITY #5*	*DAY SEVEN* *ACTIVITY #6*	*DAY EIGHT* *ACTIVITY #6*	*DAY NINE* *UNIT SUMMARY*	*DAY TEN*
(1) Continue Activity #5. (2) Team members continue rehearsing scene segments. (3) Help actors find appropriate props and costumes if necessary. (4) Students should schedule a performance date with teacher for day eight, nine, or ten. (5) Talent Day should be tentatively planned for day ten or eleven.	(1) Continue Activity 6. Final rehearsal day for pre-blocked scene. (2) Team members continue rehearsing scene segments. (3) Group members/viewers offer suggestions and share props.	(1) Continue Activity #6. Final performances of pre-blocked scenes. (2) Viewers offer positive feedback.	(1) Continue Activity #6. Final performances of pre-blocked scenes. (2) Viewers offer positive feedback. (3) If all groups have completed performances, have students read aloud the Unit Summary at end of Unit Five. Have a student read aloud the ten skills learned in Unit Five. Students benefit from reviewing the skills learned in each unit.	(1) If needed, use day ten for final scene performances. (2) Talent Day gives actors the opportunity to perform and shine. (3) Unit Five Talent Day information is *not* printed in the *Student Handbook*. It appears only in this *Teacher's Guide*. (4) If you decide to have Talent Day on day ten or eleven, announce your decision to the class on day five. Then offer the choices for Talent Day printed in this *Teacher's Guide*.

WEEK AT A GLANCE: WEEK TWO

ACTIVITY #1

Stage Terms: Commentary
Stage Areas & Actors' Body Positions

ONE Exercise A appears only in this *Teacher's Guide*. It does not appear in the *Student Handbook*.

TWO Vocabulary is best learned through experience rather than printed definitions. Directors can effectively teach concepts like **opening up to an audience, dressing the stage,** and **making a triangle** during the normal rehearsal process. Teach a brief lesson on stage terminology. Then allow students to make discoveries on their own.

THREE This unit deals with vocabulary related to stage areas, stage abbreviations, body positions, and blocking. The first set of terms in the *Student Handbook* define **stage areas**. The diagram is more effective than a list of definitions. Reinforce the students' understanding of the terms with three volunteers on-stage.

> *Vocabulary is best learned through experience rather than printed definitions.*

STAGE AREAS

Upstage	Stage Left	Curtain Line
Downstage	Stage Center	Off-stage
Stage Right	Apron	Wings

FOUR On the floor, mark stage areas with chalk prior to class. Preparation saves class time. Students experience success when they can quickly begin a well-planned exercise.

FIVE The second set of terms in the *Student Handbook* deals with actors' body positions. The diagram is more effective than a list of definitions. Reinforce the students' understanding of the terms with three volunteers on stage.

ACTORS' BODY POSITIONS

EXERCISE A

Stage Terms and Actors' Body Positions

Purpose:

Students learn stage terms and actors' body positions through experience on stage.

Execution:

ONE Arbitrarily select three students. Have students stand on chalk-marked areas on the stage. In that way, students learn the terms as they move from space to space.

TWO From the audience call stage directions as follows:

• Bob, stand **Down Left.**

• Sally, stand **Up Center.**

- George, stand **Right of Center.**

- Now, Bob, move to the **Up Left** of George so that you are standing between George and Sally.

- Sally, move **Down Left** four steps.

- George, move **straight down** two steps.

THREE Ask audience members to identify the stage areas in which each of the volunteers is now standing. Repeat the process, using other volunteers. Allow class members to give directions to the actors.

FOUR The second set of terms, the abbreviations, do not require discussion. They are provided as a reference for students when they are working with the three pre-blocked scenes. Explain that acting editions of plays from publishers like Samuel French often use these same abbreviations.

...acting editions of plays from publishers like Samuel French often use these same abbreviations.

FIVE ABBREVIATIONS USED BY ACTORS AND PLAYWRIGHTS

C.	= Center Stage	R.C.	= Right Center
D.	= Downstage or toward the audience	S.L.	= Stage Left
D.C.	= Downstage Center	S.R.	= Stage Right
D.L.	= Downstage Left	U.	= Upstage or away from the audience
D.L.C.	= Downstage Left Center	U.C.	= Upstage Center
D.R.	= Downstage Right	U.L.	= Upstage Left
D.R.C.	= Downstage Right Center	U.L.C.	= Upstage Left Center
L.	= to the left	U.R.	= Upstage Right
L.C.	= Left Center	U.R.C.	= Upstage Right Center
R.	= to the right	X	= cross

SIX Repeat the same teaching method that you used for stage terms when teaching students about body positions.

SEVEN Arbitrarily select three students. Have the students stand on the stage. From the audience the instructor asks the volunteers to do the following:

- Anthony, stand **full back to the audience.**

- Theresa, stand **one-quarter to the audience, Stage Right.**

- William, stand **right profile to the audience.**

- Now, Anthony, stand **facing left three-quarters.**

- Theresa, stand **facing right three-quarters.**

- William, stand **left profile to the audience.**

EIGHT Repeat the process, using other volunteers. Allow class members to give directions to the actors.

NINE The terms listed in the *Student Handbook* are not meant to be a definitive list. Theatre has spawned many specific words. This book has presented the basic terminology.

ACTIVITY #2
Blocking a Scene

Purpose:

Students demonstrate a character's dominance through blocking.

Students demonstrate a character's dominance through blocking.

Preparation:

ONE Prior to Activity #2, divide your class into groups of six. Record the names of students in each group. As in past exercises, mix experienced or confident actors with shy or reluctant actors. Students build on each other's strengths.

TWO There are six students in each group, or three pairs. Several days prior to Activity #2, create a list of assigned parts for each pair of students in the designated groups. Then tell each student his/her part. Each student needs to memorize the short part before Activity #2 begins. Alert participants that they have two days to memorize their short parts. You may wish to allow each participant to choose his own part.

THREE The activity progresses quickly and successfully when students memorize their lines. Reassure students that "A Family Difference" is a one-page script. Participants experience a sense of competence and pride when they memorize their short parts. Moreover, students quickly realize that it is easier and more effective to block a scene when actors know their lines. Some instructors prefer to block scenes as the actors read their lines from the text. Use the procedure that best meets your needs.

FOUR On the day of the activity, some instructors like to separate their groups into different rooms or areas. Other teachers like to keep the groups in one environment where they can see each group on task. Again, you choose the best method to meet your needs and the needs of your students and principal.

FIVE Choose the location where you wish all five or six groups to meet at the completion of their rehearsal sessions. The area can be as simple as the middle of the room. Planning details ahead of time helps students succeed in this activity.

Execution:

ONE Direct student attention to the first two pages of Unit Five. Students read out loud the introductory material explaining blocking. Next, ask two students to read the short script, "A Family Difference," out loud. Lastly, have students read aloud the following two pages, "Blocking a Scene," and the directions for Activities #2 and #3. Students have a better understanding of an activity if they read it first.

TWO Arbitrarily assign the parts to two students. In front of the class, the two actors perform the script, "A Family Difference," from Activity #2 in the *Student Handbook*. Every student will have memorized his part prior to Activity #2. Therefore, the demonstration will proceed efficiently.

THREE With the instructor's help, audience members offer blocking suggestions for the demonstration scene, "A Family Difference." Next, in order to display the effectiveness of the blocking, demonstrators perform their newly blocked scene in front of the class. The instructor offers suggestions for more effective ways to establish dominance. Activity #2 emphasizes that the parent is the dominant character in the scene.

The instructor offers suggestions for more effective ways to establish dominance.

FOUR Divide the class into groups of six. Students block the scene focusing on the parent as the dominant character. On each team, pair #1 will choose the blocking for their interpretation of "A Family Difference." Then the second and third pair of participants will block their versions of the same scene. Students have memorized their parts prior to class. Allow twenty minutes for all three pairs to block their scenes.

FIVE As the first pair blocks its interpretation of the scene, the remaining four students function as an audience. Audience members offer suggestions to pair #1. Next, as pair #2 creates its blocking version, the other four participants become the audience. Again, audience members may contribute additional blocking suggestions. Lastly, pair #3 blocks its interpretation of "A Family Difference." The four audience members are encouraged to offer blocking suggestions.

SIX After the groups have completed Activity #1, they return to the designated meeting place. If time permits, teams demonstrate their blocking choices for Activity #2. If no time remains, students will continue the demonstration session on the following day. At that time, participants will demonstrate their blocking versions for Activities #2 and #3.

SEVEN Participants discuss their choice of blocking solutions.

- Audience members identify specific blocking choices that helped establish dominance.

- Audience members identify vocal variations that helped establish dominance.

- Audience members recall relative body positions that made one character stronger than the other.

The instructor can offer further blocking suggestions for each group's blocking solution.

ACTIVITY #3

Re-Blocking "A Family Difference"

Purpose:

Students reveal a character's dominance through blocking.

Students reveal a character's dominance through blocking.

Execution:

ONE Students remain in the same groups. Focusing on the child as the dominant character, students re-block the scene. On each team, pair #1 initially will choose the blocking for its new interpretation of "A Family Difference." Then the second and third pair of participants will block their versions of the same scene. Allow twenty minutes for all three pairs to block their scenes.

TWO As the first pair blocks its interpretation of the scene, the remaining four students function as an audience. Audience members offer suggestions to pair #1. Next, as pair #2 creates its blocking version, the other four participants become the audience. Again, audience members may contribute additional blocking suggestions. Lastly, pair #3 blocks its interpretation of "A Family Difference." The four audience members are encouraged to offer blocking suggestions.

THREE After the groups have completed Activity #3, they return to the designated meeting place. Participants demonstrate their blocking versions for Activity #3. Participants discuss their choice of blocking solutions.

FOUR Audience members identify specific blocking choices that helped establish dominance. Audience members identify vocal variations that helped establish dominance. Audience members recall relative body positions that made one character stronger than the other. The instructor can offer further blocking suggestions for each group's blocking solution. Remember to praise the strongest moments in each scene.

Remember to praise the strongest moments in each scene.

SCRIPTS AND THE PROBLEMS THEY MAY PRESENT

At times, theatre activities may require that each student read an entire one-act play or a complete scene prior to class. Therefore, each student will need his own copy of the script or text. Many schools purchase classroom sets of short plays and scene books such as: *Fifteen American One-Act Plays*, Paul Kozelka, editor; *More Scenes That Happen,* by Mary Krell-Oishi, and *Two-character Plays for Student Actors* by Robert Mauro. Numerous other texts and booklets are available for school districts to purchase at a nominal cost for their students.

In Activity #3 you may want your students to read an entire scene of your choosing. This reading assignment may pose a problem for some teachers. **It is against the law for anyone to make and distribute copies of any copyrighted scripts (or entire copyrighted printed chapters) without written permission from a publisher.** If you are in doubt whether you can copy a particular item, call the publisher.

ACTIVITY #4

Commentary

Activity #4 concentrates on three pre-blocked scenes. The first two scenes have been excerpted from the humorous English play, *Box and Cox* by John Madison Morton. *Box and Cox* is a comedy of coincidences. The third scene comes from a translation of the Russian play, *The Bear,* also called *The Boor,* by Anton Chekhov.

Both comedies were written over 100 year ago before copyrights were established. These plays are in the public domain. Like plays by William Shakespeare, works in the public domain are not covered by copyright law. However, some adaptations and translations *are* copyrighted works. If you ever have questions about works in the public domain, consult a librarian about your legal responsibilities.

The first time you teach activity #3, you may wish to have your students just read and perform the three pre-blocked scene segments as they appear in the *Student Handbook.* However, some instructors want their students to read the entire play from which these scenes have been excerpted.

Activity #4 incorporates many skills that students have learned in earlier lessons. Now participants gain further experience in matching actions to words. Because the scenes have been carefully blocked beforehand, most of those actions are necessary actions. However, there is room for interpretive actions also. In addition, students become more conscious of the stage pictures contained within the scene. Activity #4 also provides added opportunities to work with specialized stage terminology and to practice memorization skills.

In Activity #4 a new concept is introduced: the analysis of a character's motives. Actors develop good character analysis skills by reading plays. They also refine these skills through practice.

Because memorization is involved in Activity #3, you may wish to plan ahead now. Begin to think about how you will divide your class into groups. One week prior to Activity #3, you need to assign parts from the pre-blocked scene segments to each student. *Box and Cox* (opening scene) has parts for one female and one male. *Box and Cox* (scene two) has parts for two males. Lastly, *The Bear* has parts for one female and two males.

All three scene segments lend themselves to nontraditional casting. There are more male characters than females in the three scenes. Consider casting females in male roles. (1) The servant, Luka, in the play *The Bear* could be played by a female. (2) The characters Box and Cox can be played by two females. The females can play the parts as female characters or as male characters. Read the play segments so that you are familiar with the characters.

> **If you ever have questions about works in the public domain, consult a librarian about your legal responsibilities.**

ONE Prior to Activity #4, divide your class into groups of six or seven, considering the characters in each play. (See the following casting list for the three scene segments.) Record the names of students in each group. All participants in a group will perform the same previously blocked scene segment. Students work in pairs. Therefore, there will be three pairs in each group. Mix experienced or confident actors with shy or reluctant actors. Students build on each other's talents.

TWO Following is a casting form for you to use when dividing your class into groups of six to seven students.

Role Assignments for Three Pre-Blocked Scenes

TEAM ONE: female = f   male = m

Box and Cox — Scene One

A. MRS. BOUNCER (f) _____ COX (m) _____

B. MRS. BOUNCER (f) _____ COX (m or f) _____

C. MRS. BOUNCER (f) _____ COX (m or f) _____

TEAM TWO: female = f   male = m

Box and Cox — Scene Two

D. BOX (m) _____ COX (m) _____

E. BOX (m or f) _____ COX (m or f) _____

F. BOX (m or f) _____ COX (m or f) _____

TEAM THREE: female = f   male = m

The Bear — Scene Three

G. SMIRNOV (m) _____ POPOVA (f) _____

H. SMIRNOV (m) _____ POPOVA (f) _____

I. SMIRNOV (m) _____ POPOVA (f) _____

and LUKA (m or f) _____

THREE Assign Team One: Scene One of *Box and Cox*. Depending upon the makeup of your class, this team can consist of: (a) 3 males and 3 females; (b) 2 males and 4 females; or (c) 1 male and 5 females. Nontraditional casting can be challenging and enjoyable for actors.

Nontraditional casting can be challenging and enjoyable for actors.

Assign Team Two: Scene Two of *Box and Cox*. Depending upon the makeup of your class, this team can consist of six males, four males and two females, or two males and four females. Again, stress to students that nontraditional casting can be challenging and enjoyable for actors — especially in a comedy.

Assign Team Three: Scene Three of *The Bear*. Depending upon the makeup of your class, this team can consist of four males and three females, three males and four females, or three males and three females. The third character in this scene is an old servant named Luka. Luka can be played by a female or male. The same person can act in all three performances for her team. Or, if the class is small, the character, Luka, can be cut from the scene.

FOUR Create a list of assigned parts for each pair of students in each group. Then tell each student his/her part. Ask students to memorize their short parts before Activity #4 begins. Alert participants that they have one week to memorize their parts.

FIVE The activity moves quickly, easily, and successfully when students memorize their lines. Participants experience a sense of competence and pride in themselves when they memorize their parts.

Participants experience a sense of competence and pride in themselves when they memorize their parts.

SIX Some instructors like to separate their groups into different rooms or areas. Other teachers like to keep the groups in one environment where they can see each group on task. Again, you choose the best method to meet your needs and the needs of your students and principal.

SEVEN Choose the location where you wish all five or six groups to meet at the completion of their acting and blocking sessions. The area can be as simple as the middle of the room. Planning details ahead of time helps students succeed in this activity.

EIGHT PROPS: For all three pre-blocked scenes.

Help students locate rehearsal props. After assigning each student a part, give teams a list of props needed for their scene segment.

In *Box and Cox*, Scene One — Cox will need: a mirror, hairbrush, razor for shaving, a dictionary, and four hats. Mrs. Bouncer has no props.

In *Box and Cox,* Scene Two — Cox will need: a letter and an envelope. Box has no props.

In *The Bear,* Scene Three — Popova will need the following props: a pistol case (you could use the case for a musical instrument), and two wooden toy pistols. These do not need to be realistic. Smirnov has no props. Luka, the older servant, has no props.

NINE COSTUMES: For all three pre-blocked scenes.

Help students locate appropriate simple costumes. After assigning each student a part, give teams a list of appropriate, simple apparel needed for their scene segment.

Male actors need to locate appropriate trousers/suit, or a bulky sweater/brown blazer. The actors playing Cox need to pin their suit jackets to make them look more old-fashioned. Cox also wears a formal necktie. Box, the printer, might wear a brown bulky sweater, tweed jacket, and trousers. Smirnov might wear boots, work trousers, a turtleneck shirt, and a Russian fur cap. Luka, the elderly servant, is described below.

Female participants should go to the costume room or to their home closets and find apparel that may be appropriate. Mrs. Bouncer might wear an ankle-length dress, an apron, and an Amish-type cap. Popova might wear a stylish ankle-length dress, some jewelry, and some stylish shoes from the late 1800s. Students can cleverly adapt modern clothes and shoes to give the appearance of apparel from the late 1800s. Luka, the elderly servant, would wear dark clothes, an apron, and black shoes. Actors need to wear suitable footwear. Tennis shoes are not appropriate for actors to wear.

TEN Decide if your students will perform before an invited audience. If that is the case, then invite audience members now. Student actors gain immeasurable skills, rehearse more seriously, and take greater pride in their work when they perform before an audience. Possible audiences could be other theatre or English classes and invited family members.

Student actors gain immeasurable skills, rehearse more seriously, and take greater pride in their work when they perform before an audience.

EXERCISE A

Purpose:

Students learn several methods for memorizing information.

Many people believe that memorizing anything is difficult. But that is not true.

Preparation:

ONE Exercise A and B appear only in this *Teacher's Guide*. The *Student Handbook* does not contain Exercise A and B or the following homework assignment.

TWO HOMEWORK ASSIGNMENT: Ask students to read the nine tips for memorizing dialog. Have students informally list five different facts that they memorize daily. Some ideas for their lists could be phone numbers, addresses, shopping lists, friends' addresses, answers for short tests, song lyrics, menus at restaurants, prices for clothing items, titles of popular songs, and actors' names and the movies in which they appeared. Everyone memorizes something almost every day.

THREE This section deals with ways in which everyone can memorize information, particularly script dialog. Ask students to examine why it is easy to memorize certain facts. Instructors need to consider this concept also. Many people believe that memorizing anything is difficult. But that is not true.

FOUR People, young and old, memorize things every day. At times a person worries that he cannot remember and recall information that he once knew. Relax. Everyone has trouble recalling facts at some point.

FIVE Brains are like computers. We learn new facts and ideas constantly. We store the new information in our minds. Our brains are crammed with concepts we have learned during our entire life. However, remember: all of the memorized information stays in our mind. We just have to find ways to recall it.

Execution:

ONE Have students read out loud the nine tips for memorizing dialog. Ask individual students to explain each tip.

TWO Do any of the tips apply to other subjects and areas? For example, is it easier to remember class notes if certain words and sentences are highlighted with a pen? Whenever someone wants to remember a phone number, does that person repeat the number several times?

THREE Ask each student to share his/her prepared list describing different facts one memorizes every day. Are some facts or ideas easier to memorize than others? If a person is interested in something, is it easier to learn and remember? Is it more difficult to memorize information if a person is not interested in the subject?

EXERCISE B

Purpose:

Students learn about a character's motives and how motives affect an actor's interpretation of the part. Students review and understand the seven goals for successful completion of this activity.

Execution:

ONE Exercise B appears only in this *Teacher's Guide.* The *Student Handbook* does not contain Exercise B.

TWO Have the class read out loud the section titled "Acting a Pre-Blocked Scene." Then, direct student attention to Activity #4 — "Performing a Pre-Blocked Scene Segment."

THREE Students read aloud the directions for Activity #4. Pay particular attention to direction #1 which instructs students to read aloud the scene synopses and seven goals.

FOUR FRENCH SCENES: This is a good time to explain the term **French scenes.** When classical French plays were first published, each fragment, noted by an entrance or an exit, was labeled a separate scene. Therefore, a French scene is a fragment of a scene. The end or the beginning of a French scene occurs whenever a character leaves the stage or a new character enters.

FIVE Some directors like to divide their analysis of a play script into French scenes. For each French scene they ask: "Who is the main character on stage in this scene?" The answer to that question aids the director and actors in deciding how to arrange characters. They want the strongest focus on the most important character.

SIX A **beat** may be described as a character's subtle feeling or a change in his/her own motives. Beats can occur in the middle of an actor's line. Or a beat can occur after another actor responds. Each actor must closely examine his/her own changing motives.

A beat may be described as a character's subtle feeling or a change in his/her own motives.

ACTIVITY #5

Performing a Pre-Blocked Scene
Part One

Students rehearse a short scene segment and practice memorizing techniques.

Purpose:

Students rehearse a short scene segment and practice memorizing techniques.

Execution:

ONE To the class, read the following background information for each of the three scene segments. You may wish to read these same synopses to the audience on the days that the class performs.

Box and Cox, Scene One — *Box and Cox* is a comedy of farcical coincidences. It takes place in Mrs. Bouncer's house in London. Mrs. Bouncer is trying to earn extra money by renting the same room to both Mr. Cox, a person who makes hats, and to Mr. Box, a printer. Mr. Cox works days and returns to his room at night. Mr. Box works nights and returns to his room during the day. When the scene opens, Cox, in his shirtsleeves, is viewing his hair in a small mirror that he holds in his hand. Mrs. Bouncer is in his room. Both Cox and Box believe that their room is vacant when they are at work. They do not know that Mrs. Bouncer has rented the same room to both of them.

Box and Cox, Scene Two — This scene segment takes place later in the play. Box and Cox have met and learned that Mrs. Bouncer has rented the same room to both men. Box and Cox also discover that both of them have proposed marriage to the same person, a widow named Penelope Ann Wiggins. She has sued both Box and Cox for breach of promise. Both Box and Cox hope that they will never see the widow Penelope Ann again. As the second scene begins, Mrs. Bouncer has just delivered a letter from Margate, a beach side town where the widow Wiggins runs a profitable business.

The Bear, Scene Three — This scene is adapted from a one-act play by the Russian author Anton Chekhov. The title, *The Bear,* is sometimes translated as *The Boor.* In the story, Popova is a pretty young widow who owns a farm. She still is in mourning seven months after the death of her husband. Smirnov is the owner of a neighboring farm. Popova's late husband had owed Smirnov a large amount of money for oats. Smirnov has pushed his way into Popova's house. He had demanded that Popova pay him the interest on his loan. Popova has said that she will pay him the day after tomorrow. They have argued. Smirnov has been shouting, stomping around the room, and bullying Luka, Popova's elderly servant. Smirnov has been insulting women in general, and Popova in particular. Popova finally has become angry. She is trying to get Smirnov out of her house.

TWO Divide the class into three teams. Each team will have six actors. Team members read their assigned scene. Participants read out loud, round robin style. Round robin style means no one is assigned a specific character to read. Instead, the actors are seated in a circle. Going around the circle, they take turns reading the parts in the play. Each participant reads part of the time. Then she must follow the script with her eyes the remainder of the time.

THREE Give each group masking tape and a yardstick. All six participants tape the ground plan of their scene on the floor of their small rehearsal area. Groups do not require big rehearsal spaces. Great acting and blocking is not determined by large or expensive surroundings.

FOUR Students on each team rehearse their assigned memorized scene segments. Initially, two students on each team will walk through the assigned scene as a demonstration for their team members. They will follow the blocking written in the right hand margin of the script. Then the second and third pair of students will walk through the same blocking of the same scene. Allow thirty minutes for all three pairs to walk through their scenes.

FIVE As the first pair interprets the blocking written in the margin of their assigned segment from the *Student Handbook*, the remaining four students function as an audience. Audience members offer suggestions to pair #1. Then, as pair #2 walks through its blocking version, the other four participants become the audience. Again, audience members may offer suggestions to the actors. Lastly, pair #3 practices its interpretation of the same scene. The four audience members are encouraged to offer further acting suggestions.

SIX The instructor visits each group as it rehearses and blocks its scene segment. The instructor, acting as director, provides guidance and blocking interpretations to each group.

Great acting and blocking is not determined by large or expensive surroundings.

SEVEN INSTRUCTOR COMMENTS

- Call attention to the motives of the characters.

- Note how knowledge of motive influences the rate of delivery, voice quality, posture, and intensity of a character's gaze.

- Does a character's motive shift? In what way?

- Use stage terminology when it seems appropriate: Down Left Center, One-Quarter Profile Right, and Three-Quarters Left.

- Refer to concepts and techniques that have been stressed in earlier exercises: shifting motives, necessary actions, interpretive actions.

- Students need to do more than memorize lines and move mechanically around a stage area.

- Students should aim for an understanding of the author's words.

> *Students should aim for an understanding of the author's words.*

EIGHT Remind students about props for all three scene segments. Help the teams locate props for their particular scene segment. Actors in each group can share some of the props and have duplicates of others.

In *Box and Cox,* Scene One — Cox will need a mirror, hairbrush, razor for shaving, a dictionary, and four hats. Mrs. Bouncer has no props.

In *Box and Cox,* Scene Two — Cox will need a letter and an envelope. Box has no props.

In *The Bear,* Scene Three — Popova will need a pistol case (you could use the case for a musical instrument), and toy wooden pistols. Smirnov has no props. Luka, the older servant, has no props.

NINE Remind students about suitable costumes for all three pre-blocked segments. Help students locate appropriate simple costumes. After assigning each student a part, give each team a list of appropriate, simple clothes needed for their particular scene segment.

Male actors need to locate appropriate trousers/suit, and a bulky sweater/brown blazer. The actors playing Cox need to pin their suit jackets to make them look more old-fashioned. Cox also wears a formal necktie. Box, the printer, might wear a brown bulky sweater, tweed jacket, and trousers. Smirnov might wear boots, work trousers, a turtleneck shirt, and a Russian fur cap. Luka, the elderly servant, is described below.

Female participants should go to the costume room or to their home closets and find apparel that may be appropriate. Mrs. Bouncer might wear an ankle-length dress, an apron, and an Amish-type cap. Popova might wear a stylish ankle-length dress, some jewelry, and some stylish shoes from the late 1800s. Students can cleverly adapt modern clothes and shoes to give the appearance of apparel from the late 1800s. Luka, the elderly servant, would wear dark clothes, an apron, and black shoes. Actors need to wear suitable footwear. Tennis shoes are not appropriate for actors to wear.

TEN Schedule a day for each team's performance of their pre-blocked scenes. Inquire whether all actors have their necessary props and costumes. Offer assistance in locating needed items.

ACTIVITY #6

Performing a Pre-blocked Scene
Part Two

Purpose:

Students continue to rehearse their short pre-blocked scene segments and to practice memorizing techniques.

Execution:

ONE Students continue to rehearse their pre-blocked scenes in the areas in which they have been assigned. Each team should critique and help its members on their presentations.

TWO Students should be using their appropriate props during these rehearsals. In addition, encourage students to wear their costumes or parts of the costume. Costumes and props often help actors prepare their roles more effectively.

THREE Visit each group as actors rehearse. Encourage team members to offer positive suggestions.

FOUR Have all groups convene during the last ten minutes of the class. Remind students of their performance day. Inquire whether all actors have their necessary props and costumes. Offer assistance in locating needed items.

Students continue to rehearse their short pre-blocked scene segments and to practice memorizing techniques.

FIVE Remind students of the invited audience members if students will be performing for nonclass members.

ACTIVITY #7

Final Performances

Purpose:

Students perform a short segment of a play before an audience of class members and possibly other audience members.

Execution:

ONE Today is the day of reckoning. Students perform their short scene segments before an audience.

TWO Before the performance, read the background information for each of the three pre-blocked scene segments to audience members. Activity #3 of Unit Five contains a brief synopsis of each scene.

Describe the layout of the set. It will exist mostly in the actors' and viewers' imaginations, rather than through the use of flats and set pieces. Ask audience members to reserve all comments about a scene until all the pairs of actors have performed.

Focus on interpretation variations that help to reveal motive.

Invite audience members to explain the characters' motives. Focus on interpretation variations that help to reveal motive. Ask students to consider factors that contribute to the success of the actors' performances. Actors need to hear that someone noticed an inflection, pause, or a subtle gesture. Actors use them to develop characterization.

THREE Unit Five introduced several theatre terms and stage movement concepts. Some teachers may want to assess student understanding of this information after the performances. A unit test on stage terms follows the Unit Summary.

TALENT DAY

The following Talent Day information is printed only in this *Teacher's Guide*. Unlike Unit Three, the Talent Day choices are not printed in the *Student Handbook*. You decide whether Talent Day is appropriate for your class in Unit Five.

Unit Five activities gave students the opportunity to make choices and to perform. In theatre, an actress needs to practice her craft constantly. She needs opportunities to perform. Talent Day gives the actor experience in performing before an audience. Participants have a chance to shine! Following are several choices for Talent Day — Unit Five that you may wish to offer to your students:

- Find a poem, monolog or short passage that you like. Present it as an oral interpretation reading.

- Find a short or funny sketch. Rehearse the scene. Memorize the lines. Present it in front of the class.

- Choose a scene segment from any text. Many publishers sell texts containing scenes for performing as well as one-act plays. Perform the scene before the class.

- Expand *Box and Cox* or *The Bear*. Include a longer segment of the actual script.

UNIT SUMMARY

In Units One and Two participants used improvisation to perform scenes. Students created words and actions at the same time. In Unit Five students learned that the words are written as scripts first by the author. The actors' main objective is to make those scripts and words come alive. Actors make words come alive through the choice of appropriate actions.

Following is a list of ten skills participants learned in this unit:

1. Students learned to read scripts carefully.

2. Students learned to understand stage movement terms and concepts.

3. Students learned to identify different directing techniques.

4. Students learned to self-block a short dramatic scene.

5. Students learned to use stage movement to suggest the dominance of one character in a short scene.

6. Students learned to act in a pre-blocked scene.

7. Students learned to use a director's marginal notes.

In theatre, an actress needs to practice her craft constantly. She needs opportunities to perform.

Students learned to memorize more effectively.

8. Students learned to memorize more effectively.

9. Students learned to mark a stage floor for rehearsal.

10. Students learned to find and use suitable props in a play.

UNIT TEST

Unit Five introduced several theatre terms and stage movement concepts. Some teachers may want to assess student understanding of this information. The following questions can be used either as a unit test or as part of a semester exam. Choose how you wish to score the quiz.

Short Answer Questions:

The first seven questions refer to the following diagrams. Assume that "X" and "Y" are actors who have been positioned on a stage ground plan which divides the acting space into nine areas.

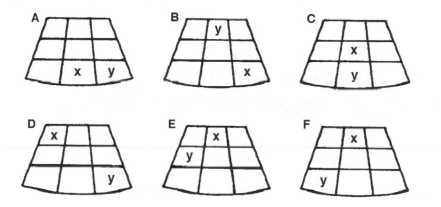

(Circle the choice which best answers each of the questions below.)

1. Which diagram shows Actor X positioned in a STAGE RIGHT area?

    a   b   c   d

2. Which of the above diagrams shows an actor positioned DOWN LEFT?

    d, e, and f   a, b, and d   a, c, and f

3. Which of the above diagrams shows Actor Y positioned UP CENTER?

    b   c   d   e

4. Which of the above diagrams shows one actor blocking another?

    a   b   c   d

5. Which diagram most closely illustrates a "shared scene"?

    a   b   c   d

6. In which diagram is Actor Y in a more dominant Upstage position in relation to Actor X?

    b   d   e   f

7. In which diagram is Actor X positioned closest to the proscenium?

    b   c   d   e

8. Which of the following positions is the strongest that an actor can have on stage?

    a. full front   b. one-quarter

    c. profile   d. three-quarter

9. Which body position is the weakest for an actor on stage?

    a. one-quarter   b. profile

    c. three-quarter   d. full back

10. If an actor is standing on the APRON of a stage, which of the following statements is most accurate?

    a. The actor is not visible to the audience.

    b. He is on a raised platform above other actors.

    c. He is on the part of the stage that is nearest the audience.

    d. He is off to one side of the stage.

11. Which of the following statements is true about performances on a thrust stage?

    a. Most of the acting is done on an extended apron.

    b. The audience surrounds the stage on three sides.

    c. Sometimes the actors can make entrances and exits down the aisles through the audience.

    d. All of the above.

12. What term is practically synonymous with "arena theatre"?

    a. theatre-in-the-round

    b. thrust theatre

    c. circus

    d. wings

13. If a stage direction in a script says an actor should be "standing above the sofa," a reader should imagine that the actor is:

      a. on a platform of some sort

      b. standing on the sofa

      c. standing behind the sofa

      d. standing in front of the sofa

Identification Questions:

Write a short explanation or definition for each of the following seven theatre terms. Definitions should apply to *theatre* only.

Blocking _____

_____

Cross _____

_____

Stage Turn_____

Upstage_____

_____

Ground Plan _____

_____

Motive _____

_____

French Scene _____

_____

Reading and Analyzing Plays

Unit Six concentrates on reading and analyzing plays. The play script is written for actors. Actors read and interpret the writer's ideas — with the help of the director. They read carefully so that they can give a believable performance. In order to give meaning to a writer's words, the actor needs to become a skillful reader of plays. Therefore, the actor must learn to develop good reading skills.

Plays are a paradox, a contradiction. They are a special form of literature. Plays are not complete when published. They are missing the actors, scenery, and movement. Plays are not written to be read by the audience. Playwrights prefer that people see their works performed rather than read them.

This unit offers students play reading techniques. Secondly, it offers literary terms for actors to consider when analyzing a play. Lastly, Unit Six offers a list of helpful questions an actor should ask himself after reading a play.

Students learn that:

- Actors need to develop careful reading skills.

- Conscientious reading helps actors learn about a character's motivation.

- An actor must fully understand a character in order to give a good performance.

- Thorough reading helps actors identify dramatic conflicts within a play.

A weekly calendar summarizing daily lessons follows. The calendar format is provided for your convenience so that you can quickly review each week's activities ahead of time or give a copy of your weekly syllabus to your principal or department chairperson.

> *In order to give meaning to a writer's words, the actor needs to become a skillful reader of plays.*

UNIT SIX: READING AND ANALYZING PLAYS

MONDAY	TUESDAY	WEDNESDAY	THURSDAY	FRIDAY
DAY ONE *ACTIVITY #1* *READING THE TEXT* (1) Students read the first page of Unit Six aloud. (2) Read aloud section "Play Reading Techniques." (3) Next, read and discuss "Visualizing a Script." (4) Follow the lesson plan in the *Teacher's Guide*. Have students visualize people, food, and flowers. Have students imagine the smell or taste of an object. (5) Ask students for examples of suggested Unit Six skills used in previous units. (6) If time allows, begin Activity #2.	*DAY TWO* *ACTIVITY #2* *LITERARY TERMS* (1) Activity #2: Students read aloud the two-page section titled "Play Analysis: Getting Started." (2) Review literary terms listed in this section. (3) Write the following words on the board: movement, liveliness, rapport, and eye contact. Briefly discuss these terms. Students implemented these skills in previous units. (4) If time allows, begin Activity #3.	*DAY THREE* *ACTIVITY #3* *"THE NOSE TREE"* (1) Activity #3: Students learn literary terms by performing the children's play "The Nose Tree." Play is printed in the Appendix of the *Student Handbook*. (2) Select two students to mark acting area with tape. Place sitting cubes. (3) Select two other students to read Narrator #1 and #2. These same actors seat audience class members. (4) Narrators read their lines. (5) Follow detailed lesson plan outlined in the *Teacher's Guide*. (6) Ask teacher questions from instructions.	*DAY FOUR* *ACTIVITY #4* *MORE LITERARY* *TERMS* (1) Begin Activity #4. Follow the directions in the *Teacher's Guide*. (2) Students read aloud pages titled "More Terms: Plot and Characterization." (3) Next, students read aloud section titled "Asking Questions About the Characters." (4) Write four literary terms on the board: plot, dramatic conflict, motivation, and spine. (5) Next, write melodrama, satire, farce, and parody. Explain meanings of terms.	*DAY FIVE* *WRAP-UP DAY &* *UNIT SUMMARY* (1) Many teachers take two days to complete Activity #3. (2) In that case, use Day Five to complete Activity #4. (3) Have students read out loud the Unit Summary for Unit Six. (4) Have a student read the nine skills learned in this unit. Students benefit from reviewing the skills learned in each unit.

WEEK AT A GLANCE: WEEK ONE

ACTIVITY #1

Play Reading Techniques for Actors

Purpose:

Actors learn play reading and visualization techniques.

Preparation:

ONE Activity #1, Activity #2, Activity #3, and Activity #4 appear only in this *Teacher's Guide*. These activities do not appear in the *Student Handbook*.

TWO Review the first four pages in Unit Six. Students will read these pages out loud in class.

THREE Actors need to learn to visualize pictures in their minds for the words they read. Several techniques work successfully. Actors can close their eyes and see an object or a person or a stage set. They can visualize a character walking across the stage.

FOUR It is easier to imagine what the actors are doing if students have seen live performances. Encourage students to see plays. High schools, middle schools, and community theatres are good places to see live theatre. Actors who attend plays are better script readers. They are able to "stage" a play in their minds. Watching live plays helps students become better actors.

FIVE TIPS TO HELP ACTORS VISUALIZE A SCRIPT: Some people have a difficult time visualizing dialog in print. They cannot picture the gestures and facial expressions. The *Student Handbook* describes in detail four tips for actors who want to remember the dramatic moments in a play script. Preview this section of Unit Six prior to teaching the lesson.

Execution:

ONE Take turns reading out loud the first page in Unit Six in the *Student Handbook*.

TWO Continue reading aloud the section titled "Play Reading Techniques for Actors." Students will have a better understanding of a concept if they read it aloud.

THREE Continue reading aloud the section titled "Visualizing a Script." Discuss the four tips. Are these sugges-

> *It is easier to imagine what the actors are doing if students have seen live performances. Encourage students to see plays.*

tions familiar to the students? Did the actors experience some of these skills in Units Three, Four, and Five?

FOUR Encourage students to imagine a pizza, visualize two people playing cards, and see a red carnation on a man's lapel.

FIVE Ask participants to recall everything about the carnation. Students need to look at the flower with their minds. How does a red carnation smell? Next, ask actors to visualize a piece of pizza. Can they see it? Can they smell it? Describe the smells. Seeing images in your mind involves senses other than sight.

SIX A brain is like a television set without the screen. Actors learn to develop their imaginations. They already can recall faces, objects, and food.

SEVEN Ask the students for specific examples of skills suggested in this unit that were implemented in previous units. Actors read a script out loud. Actors listen to other actors' voices and emotions in order to understand a character. Actors find it helpful to move on stage in an appropriate manner. These activities help actors understand their characters. Actors visualize in their minds their characters' behavior, their facial expressions, and the set.

EIGHT Explain to students that: Acting is fun. But acting is serious work. Successful actors develop good reading skills *and* good acting skills. Excellent reading and acting skills go hand in hand.

Acting is fun. But acting is serious work. Successful actors develop good reading skills and good acting skills.

ACTIVITY #2
Learning Literary Terms

Purpose:

Students learn the meaning of four main literary terms and how they apply to acting and interpreting the meaning of a script.

Execution:

ONE Review the section titled "Play Analysis: Getting Started." Review the literary terms listed in the two-page section.

TWO In order to understand plays clearly, students need to learn the four literary terms: **style, theme, mood,** and **tone.**

- **STYLE:** Is the play a drama? a farce? a melodrama? a satire? a mystery? a parody? a musical play? a musical comedy?

- **THEME:** It is the main idea of the play that the writer wants the audience to remember.

- **MOOD:** It is a term that helps define a play's general atmosphere.

- **TONE:** It is a term that describes the attitude or point of view of a script.

THREE Have students read these pages out loud in class. Students have a better understanding of the terms if they read the information out loud. Prepare to discuss the information with the students.

FOUR In addition, write the words "movement," "liveliness," "rapport," and "eye contact" on the board. These actor behaviors help define the mood or tone of a play.

FIVE Students have encountered some of these terms in the activities in Units Three, Four, and Five. Ask students in what ways does eye contact enhance an actor's performance. How does actor liveliness influence an audience? Does an actor's movement on stage influence the audience's understanding of the words in a script?

Students have a better understanding of the terms if they read the information out loud.

ACTIVITY #3

Applying Play Analysis Skills
The Nose Tree

Purpose:

Actors learn to ask themselves about the mood, style, and tone of the play. *The Nose Tree* is a children's play. Actors quickly identify the rhyming language, the fantasy, the informal style, and tone of this play.

Preparation:

ONE Prior to Activity #3, divide your class into groups of four. Record the names of students in each group. As in past exercises, mix experienced or confident actors with shy or reluctant actors. Students build on one another's talent.

TWO For your convenience, Activity #3 focuses on the first two pages of the children's play, *The Nose Tree*. This play is printed in the Appendix of the *Student Handbook*. Any classroom set of texts containing scripts or one-act plays would be suitable source material for this exercise.

THREE On the day of the activity, some instructors like to separate their groups into different rooms or areas. Other teachers like to keep the groups in one environment where they can see each group on task. Again, you choose the best method to meet your needs and the needs of your students and principal.

FOUR Choose the location you wish all five or six groups to meet at the completion of Activity #3. The area can be as simple as the middle of the room. Planning details ahead of time helps students succeed in this activity.

Planning details ahead of time helps students succeed in this activity.

Execution:

ONE Direct students' attention at this time to *The Nose Tree* in the Appendix of the *Student Handbook*. Have students read out loud the introductory information on the first page of the play.

TWO Select two students to mark the acting area with masking tape or chalk as directed on the first page of the script. The same two students will place the cubes on the stage area.

THREE Select two additional participants to read the lines of Narrators #1 and #2. These two narrators will proceed to seat the audience (class members) on three sides of the classroom marked stage area.

FOUR Sitting on two cubes, Narrators #1 and #2 read their opening lines. Inform the two actors to stop at the line "In real life, she's a sweetheart." Following are several questions you may wish to ask audience members.

FIVE TEACHER QUESTIONS

- Tell me three ways in which you could add interest to this scene (movement, liveliness of speech, and eye contact with the audience).

- Direct students' attention to the words written on the board. What do they mean?

- Will this be a happy play or a sad play? How do you know that fact?

- What narrator behaviors could spark laughter in the audience?

- Why do the audience members sit on three sides of the stage?

- Which age group did the author originally consider as an audience?

- Does the age of the audience influence the blocking of this play?

- Does it influence the actors' demeanor?

- Does the age of the audience influence the actors' movements as they speak?

- Does the audience's age make it necessary for the actors to capture their attention and interest?

SIX Divide the class into groups of four. Each group will perform the same first two pages from the script *The Nose Tree*. Allow eight minutes for the groups to prepare their two pages.

SEVEN After each group has completed the exercise, they return to the designated meeting place. Each team performs its short scene interpretations.

EIGHT This technique can be used with any classroom set of texts that contains a short script or a one-act play.

ACTIVITY #4

Play Analysis: More Literary Terms

Purpose:

Actors learn to ask themselves about the plot and dramatic conflict of a play. What is the motivation and the spine of the characters in a play?

Preparation:

ONE Direct student attention to the next two pages of Unit Six. Have students read out loud the pages titled "More Terms: Plot and Characterization." Next, have students read out loud the section titled "Asking Questions About the Characters." Students will have a better understanding of a concept if they read it aloud.

TWO Write the literary terms "plot," "dramatic conflict," "motivation," and "spine" on the board. Discuss the meaning of these words and how they apply to an actor's interpretation of his/her character. Continue to use and apply these terms

> *Actors learn to ask themselves about the plot and dramatic conflict of a play. What is the motivation and the spine of the characters in a play?*

throughout the school year whenever students are preparing their roles.

THREE Write the terms melodrama, satire, farce, and parody on the board. Explain the meanings of these terms. Ask how these terms might apply to an actor's interpretation of his character. Continue to use and apply these additional terms throughout the school year whenever students are preparing their roles.

FOUR At this time, direct student attention to the section titled "Key Questions to Ask After Reading a Play."

FIVE Review the eight key questions outlined in the *Student Handbook*. Have students read the questions out loud. Explain that you will refer to these eight key questions whenever the class examines a play script for performance.

Continue to use and apply these additional terms throughout the school year whenever students are preparing their roles.

UNIT SUMMARY

Following is a list of nine concepts participants learned in this unit:

1. Initially, plays are not written to be read. Rather, plays are written to be performed.

2. Actors need to develop good reading skills in order to understand the meaning of the play.

3. Careful reading helps actors learn about character motivation.

4. An actor must understand his character in order to give a good performance.

5. Careful reading helps actors identify dramatic conflicts within a play.

6. When reading silently, actors need to visualize. They must *see* the action in a theatre in their heads.

7. Actors can join together to read plays aloud. The round robin technique of reading involves all members of a class.

8. Actors need to understand a play's theme.

9. Other literary terms will help actors discuss plays they are reading or performing. These terms are style, mood, tone, spine, and foil.

Semester Project

Unit Seven focuses on the development of an end-of-semester project that involves the entire class. Unit Seven acts as a yardstick. It measures the success of the previous units.

Theatre is a performing art. Theatre people have a goal. That goal is to communicate feelings and ideas to their audience. Therefore, it is natural for a theatre class to combine its talents and present a final performance. This final project is similar to a chorus or orchestra concert.

This chapter will discuss working together as a group; choosing performance dates; choosing a play, one-act, scene, or story to perform; choosing an audience; working cooperatively both on-stage and off-stage; and student responsibility to the group.

Inform students that the semester project constitutes thirty percent of their semester grade. In that way, students are motivated to take personal responsibility for their individual theatre roles, specialize in an area of theatre production that interests them, demonstrate a willingness to meet group needs and deadlines, practice the skills learned this semester, and provide enjoyment to family, friends, students, and other members of your community.

A weekly calendar summarizing the first week's lessons follows. Calendars for the second and third weeks have been omitted because the end-of-semester project will take different forms in different schools. You and your students need to plot your own deadlines and goals.

> *Theatre is a performing art. Theatre people have a goal. That goal is to communicate feelings and ideas to their audience.*

UNIT SEVEN: SEMESTER PROJECT

MONDAY	TUESDAY	WEDNESDAY	THURSDAY	FRIDAY
DAY ONE *ACTIVITY #1* *GETTING STARTED* (1) Activity #1 and #2 do not appear in the *Student Handbook*. They appear only in your *Teacher's Guide*. (2) Students read aloud first two pages in Unit Seven. (3) Next, students read orally section titled "Types of Performances." (4) Now students read section "Choosing an Audience." Ask students to begin to consider the kind of performance they wish to give. That decision influences the type of audience selected.	*DAY TWO* *ACTIVITY #2* *GETTING STARTED* (1) Students will also need to consider the date and place of the production. It is important to pick a time and date early in the semester. (2) Begin Activity #2. Write the purpose of Activity #2 on the board. Have students read aloud the three pages titled "Production Responsibilities." Both you and your class need to begin to think about the tasks discussed in Activity #2. Follow the detailed instructions for discussion.	*DAY THREE* *ACTIVITY #2* *CONTINUED* (1) You and your students will now decide on the type of performance you wish to present. (2) Begin to assign production responsibilities. (3) Discuss the ballots. (4) Have students read aloud the Unit Summary for Unit Seven. Students benefit from reviewing the skills learned in each unit. Unit Seven offered students the opportunity to make decisions and to work cooperatively as a unified group.	You and your class will now create the production calendars that you need for this project. Some drama classes allow three weeks for preparation. Other groups allocate more time. Some instructors schedule only eight days to prepare for this semester project. Whatever amount of time you allocate, your students will want to create individual calendars for this project.	

WEEK AT A GLANCE: WEEK ONE

ACTIVITY #1

Your End-of-Semester Project

Purpose:

Students learn to choose a performance date, choose the type of performance, and choose an audience.

Preparation:

ONE Activity #1 and Activity #2 appear only in this *Teacher's Guide*. These activities do not appear in the *Student Handbook*. During these activities students will focus on choosing a performance date, learning types of performances, and choosing an audience.

TWO Time, talent, and money: These are the major elements that will shape every end-of-semester project differently. Keeping them in mind, the teacher and the students will make some early decisions and assignments.

Time, talent, and money: These are the major elements that will shape every end-of-semester project differently.

Time

- You will need at least three weeks to complete most end-of-semester projects. Some projects will require more time.

- Setting deadlines to accomplish various tasks is essential. When you fail to have deadlines and meet them, everyone suffers.

- All workers must create a *personal calendar* for each day of the project. The calendar will describe the sequence of tasks to be accomplished and deadlines to be met.

- Make certain that you allow a reasonable amount of time to accomplish your goals. Do you have a month remaining in which to complete the project? Do you have only a few shorts weeks? Adjust the scope of your activity to fit your time frame.

Thomas Alva Edison once wrote that talent or genius is one percent inspiration and ninety-nine percent perspiration.

Talent

• Thomas Alva Edision said that talent or genius is one percent inspiration and ninety-nine percent perspiration. We evaluate our skills by those jobs we actually accomplish and finish. Everyone does a better job if he/she is interested in the project. Choose an end-of-semester project that fits the talents of your students. Students interested in design should work in that area. Theatre offers numerous jobs both on and off the stage.

Money

• How much money is available to support an *elaborate* project?

• Will your school be able to provide materials you may need in order to carry out your dreams?

• Can scripts be purchased?

• Will the school duplicate *original* plays?

• Do you need lumber?

• Are funds available for the rental of costumes or other equipment?

• Realistically speaking, what can you expect to accomplish given the *resources* that are available?

THREE Keeping these three elements in mind, the teacher and the students will make some early decisions and assignments.

• What play or scenes will you perform?

• Who will your audience be?

• Where will you perform?

• When will your performance take place?

• What responsibilities will each class member have?

ACTIVITY #1

Getting Started on End-of-Semester Project

Execution:

ONE Activity #1 and Activity #2 appear only in this *Teacher's Guide*. These activities do not appear in the *Student Handbook*. During these activities students will focus on choosing a performance date, learning types of performances, and choosing an audience.

TWO Direct students' attention to the first two pages of Unit Seven. Have students read out loud the introductory materials for "End-of-Semester Project." Next, have students read out loud the second page of the unit and the section dealing with teamwork. Students have a better understanding of a concept if they read it aloud.

THREE Next, direct students' attention to "Types of Performances." Have students read out loud the three pages concentrating on this subject. Instructors can either choose the semester project themselves, or they can involve the entire class in the project selection. If you choose the second option, you may wish to offer the group three or four possible script choices.

> *Instructors can either choose the semester project themselves, or they can involve the entire class in the project selection.*

FOUR Following is a synopsis of the description of the three different types of performances included in the *Student Handbook*. This brief overview is provided for your convenience. The complete explanation is printed in the *Student Handbook*.

Performance #1: Short on time? Is the group not quite ready to produce a short play or one-act? Try the showcase performance. In this type of production members of your class can showcase some of the scenes and improvisations they worked on during the semester.

Performance #2: The second type of presentation also involves a collection of different theatre pieces. Class members choose new pieces to study, rehearse, and perform.

Performance #3: The third type of performance involves the entire class in the presentation of a complete one-act play. Casting, coordinating, and rehearsing the one-act requires about three weeks of class time or more. This option is attractive because everybody in the class works together.

FIVE After choosing a play script, your next step is to select an audience, time, and date. There is no set order in the process of arranging a play performance. Choosing a script, finding an audience, and picking a time and date are all interrelated.

Choosing a Performance Date: The instructor and students need to choose a performance date early in the semester. Finding a good time to perform at the end of the term is often difficult. Select a date and stick to it. You will have to find an audience for whom you can perform on that date.

Choosing an Audience: Students now need to consider their audience. Have students read aloud the section titled "Choosing an Audience" in the *Student Handbook*. Instructors can either choose the audience themselves, or they can involve the entire class in the audience selection.

If you choose the second option, you may wish to offer the group two or three possible choices. For example, you may wish to perform a play for an audience of children. You may also wish to perform a comedy for older adults. Lastly, you may choose to perform a one-act for a local middle school group.

Avoid disappointment. Firmly fix a definite time and place for the performance. In that way, there will be no last-minute problems.

Picking a Time and Place: Whatever audience you choose, you need to confirm the date and time of your performance. Double check to be sure that all members of the theatre class do not have conflicting obligations. Avoid disappointment. Firmly fix a definite time and place for the performance. In that way, there will be no last-minute problems.

ACTIVITY #2

Getting Started on End-of-Semester Project

Purpose:

Students will learn to assign production responsibilities, choose the business staff, assign post performance responsibilities, and distribute post-performance ballots.

Execution:

ONE Activity #2 appears only in this *Teacher's Guide*. This activity does not appear in the *Student Handbook*.

TWO Direct students' attention to the section titled "Production Responsibilities." Read the following three pages out loud. Students will have a better understanding of a concept if they read it aloud. They also will have the opportunity to ask questions and give their opinions.

THREE ASSIGNING ACTING AND NON-ACTING RESPONSIBILITIES: If you allow the class to choose a play, there are several questions everyone needs to consider.

- Who will perform in the play or plays selected?

- Who will build the scenery?

- Who will direct?

- What about props, sound, lighting, and box office?

FOUR The following information is not included in the *Student Handbook*. It appears only in this *Teacher's Guide*. Selecting responsible people to fill the varied roles of a production is a crucial early step that the class must take.

> *Selecting responsible people to fill the varied roles of a production is a crucial early step that the class must take.*

LIST OF RESPONSIBILITIES

Possible Roles	*Brief Description*
Playwright	Author of an original scene or one-act play
Director	Responsible for blocking and guiding actors in a scene
Assistant Director	Assists teacher/director; maintains prompt script
Producer	Coordinates all segments of the project; monitors deadlines
Safety Director	Assists producer; focuses on reducing safety hazards
Lead Actor/Actress	On-stage through most of the project selection
Featured Actor	In center focus at least once during a scene
Cameo Actor	On-stage for a brief appearance; has few lines of dialog
Set Designer/Builder	Responsible for building and placement of scenery
Designer's Assistant	Helps with the building and placement of scenery

Electrical Technician	Responsible for lights, sound, special effects
Property Coordinator	Locates, organizes, keeps track of props
Graphic/Scenic Artist	Assists others needing drawing/painting skills
Costume Coordinator	Locates, sews, and takes care of costumes
Makeup Coordinator	Supervises design, purchase, and care of makeup
Business Manager	Oversees budget, transportation, expenses, ushers
Assistant Business Manager	Responsible for programs, posters, publicity
Stage Manager	Oversees all backstage operations during performances

FIVE Ask each student to state two job preferences. Then assign *two* roles to each class member.

SIX Direct student attention to the segment in the *Student Handbook* titled "Business Staff." Read this page out loud. The business side of a production includes activities such as publicity, ticket sales, and programs.

...Programs, posters, and tickets are all part of a theatre production. If you have enough workers, you may decide to create a business staff.

SEVEN Often schools do not charge admission to a class-related presentation. Therefore, you may not need tickets. However, programs, posters, and tickets are all part of a theatre production. If you have enough workers, you may decide to create a business staff. People who are assigned business responsibilities should also make a calendar which outlines deadlines for getting specific jobs done.

EIGHT Post-Performance Activities: One set of jobs you will need to perform involves post-performance cleanup. If there has been any scenery, it must be dismantled and stored. Borrowed items should be returned. Other obvious kinds of tidying up must be done. With cooperation, however, those activities should not take more than one class period.

NINE Post-Performance Ballots: Following is an example of a ballot that you might wish to give to each audience member on the day of the performance. A ballot encourages students to invite and involve their family members and their friends. Everyone benefits from attending this performance.

BALLOT

This performance is an end-of-semester project for the Theatre Arts I class. Members of the class get extra credit for every three audience members they attract to our show. Which Theatre Arts class member persuaded you to attend?

Name: _____

In addition to the above-named individual, would you like to nominate someone else for what you believe was a job well done? If so, give that person's name below:

Name: _____

Any additional comments? _____

_____

Please give this ballot to an usher.

Having a ballot motivates students to participate in the process of attracting an audience. Moreover, it provides the teacher with some feedback. The instructor can provide feedback to the class from the ballots on the day following the performance.

TEN This unit began by noting that theatre is a performing art. It then described the kinds of performances you might give. At the end, however, we have seen that a performer does not function alone. He or she must be able to rely on the contributions of a great many backstage helpers. In the end-of-semester project each student has a role to play: as an actor and as a helper providing behind-the-scenes support to other performers.

Having a ballot motivates students to participate in the process of attracting an audience.

UNIT SUMMARY

Following is a list of six skills participants learned in this unit:

1. To select appropriate material for the group to perform.

...We have seen that a performer does not function alone. He or she must be able to rely on the contributions of a great many back-stage helpers.

2. To set a production date and then stick to it.

3. To select an audience and inform them of the date.

4. To provide behind-the-scenes assistance.

5. To work cooperatively as a group in order to produce a final showcase or one-act play.

6. To give the final performance!

UNIT EIGHT
Individual Learning Activities

Unit Eight concentrates on independent learning activities for student directors. Independent learners gain valuable skills and experience in a series of directing related activities. Students learn play directing techniques and have an opportunity to apply their skills.

In Activity #1, student directors cast and direct actors in a short scene. In Activity #2, students concentrate on more complex directing activities. Student directors apply directing techniques when casting and directing fellow students in a one-act play.

In Unit Eight, students apply the following directing techniques:

- Students learn that directors need to answer many questions before tryouts.

- They learn that selecting a scene or play sometimes can be effortless. At other times the process may require research.

- Students learn that a good director gains respect by showing respect to the actors.

- They learn that thorough reading helps directors identify dramatic conflicts within a play.

- Students learn the importance of preparation before rehearsals begin.

- They learn to create a production schedule.

- Students learn to prepare a prompt script.

- Students learn to prepare for a final performance.

There is no calendar for the instructor in Unit Eight. The student director will be pursuing independent study and developing his own schedule.

Students learn that selecting a scene or play sometimes can be effortless. At other times the process may require research.

ACTIVITY #1

Directing a Short Scene

EXERCISE A

Selecting and Analyzing a Short Scene

ONE In the previous units, all activities were written for whole class participation. Unit Eight was written for individual students who wish to pursue directing.

TWO Many students express an interest in pursuing acting as a career. Fewer students choose to be directors. However, for those students who wish to gain directing experience, this unit offers several detailed, skill-oriented activities.

THREE In Activity #1, student directors gain valuable skills learning to direct a short scene.

FOUR In Exercise A, students first learn to select and analyze a scene in a series of five independent activities.

FIVE The *Student Handbook* contains an Exercise A post evaluation for student directors to complete at the conclusion of this exercise.

> **Many students express an interest in pursuing acting as a career. Fewer students choose to be directors.**

EXERCISE B

Blocking the Short Scene

ONE In Exercise B, the student director learns to block the selected scene in a series of five independent activities. In addition, students learn to develop a simple ground plan and prepare a prompt script.

TWO The *Student Handbook* contains an Exercise B post evaluation for student directors to complete at the conclusion of this exercise.

EXERCISE C

Casting and Directing the Short Scene

ONE In Exercise C, the student director casts and directs the selected short scene in a series of six independent learning activities. Students learn to plan a rehearsal schedule and cast and direct the short scene to present to classmates or a larger audience.

TWO The *Student Handbook* contains an Exercise C post evaluation for student directors to complete at the conclusion of this exercise.

ACTIVITY #2

Directing a One-Act Play

EXERCISE A

Selecting a One-Act Play

ONE In Activity #2, student directors will gain valuable skills learning to direct a one-act play. Students start at the beginning, just as a professional director would do.

TWO In Exercise A, students first learn to select a one-act play in a series of four independent activities.

THREE Your school may wish to showcase the student directed one-act plays at a school assembly.

FOUR The *Student Handbook* contains an Exercise A post evaluation for student directors to complete at the conclusion of this exercise.

EXERCISE B

Preparing for Rehearsals

ONE In Exercise B, the student director learns to prepare for rehearsals for the selected one-act play. Exercise B consists of a series of four independent activities. Students learn to develop a simple ground plan, prepare a prompt script, and create a production schedule.

TWO The *Student Handbook* contains an Exercise B post evaluation for student directors to complete at the conclusion of this exercise.

> *Students learn to develop a simple ground plan, prepare a prompt script, and create a production schedule.*

EXERCISE C

Casting, Rehearsing, and Directing the One-Act Play

ONE In Exercise C, the student director learns to prepare for rehearsals for the selected one-act play. Exercise C consists of a series of four independent activities. Student directors learn to schedule tryouts, cast the one-act play, recruit students to work in design and construction, rehearse the play, and present the one-act play for performance to classmates or a larger audience.

TWO The *Student Handbook* contains an Exercise C post evaluation for student directors to complete at the conclusion of this exercise.

The Engelsman Theatre Games

International Airport Fact Sheet

Your Character's Name: _____

Why are you at the airport? (Check one)

_____ Leaving on a trip to _____

_____ Passing through on a trip from _____ to _____

_____ Arriving from _____

_____ Meeting someone who is visiting

_____ Other_____

Are you in the waiting room alone or with someone else?

_____ Alone _____ With someone else

If you are on a trip, is it for business, pleasure, or family matters? Explain.

_____

_____

If you are on a trip, which of the following flights are you waiting to board? (Check one)

_____ TWA, Flight 750 to Chicago and Montreal

_____ Alitalia Airlines, Flight 406 to New York and Rome

_____ American Airlines, Flight 823 to Denver, Phoenix, and San Diego

_____ Delta Airlines, Flight 117 to Atlanta, Orlando, and Miami

_____ United Airlines, Flight 311 to San Francisco

_____ Other: _____

The listed flights are referred to in the public address announcements accompanying this exercise. If your destination is somewhere other than the cities mentioned, assume that the flight you checked is the first part of a longer trip. You may have to switch planes.

What luggage (if any) do you have with you?

_____

If you are not on a trip, what specific circumstances have brought you to the airport?

_____

_____

Additional background information:

How old are you? _____

Occupation: _____

Hobbies, favorite pastimes: _____

Facts about your family: _____

_____

How will you pass the time, or what will be on your mind as you sit in the waiting room? _____

Text of Public Address Announcements

Baggage from all recent incoming flights is now arriving at carousel 2. Due to the similarity of luggage, please match your claim checks with the tags on the luggage. Please present your claim check upon request.

(30 second pause)

United Airlines, Flight 311 to San Francisco, will depart from gate 20 on concourse C. All passengers for United Airlines, Flight 311 to San Francisco, please report to gate 20 for boarding.

(35 second pause)

American Airlines announces that Flight 823 to Denver, Phoenix, and San Diego has been delayed for 30 minutes. Passengers making connecting flights at Denver, Phoenix, or San Diego should check at the flight information desk...American Airlines, Flight 823, has been delayed for 30 minutes.

(50 second pause)

Will the party who left a camera at the carryon baggage security station please return and claim it.

(30 second pause)

Baggage from TWA, Flight 320, is now arriving on carousel 3. Due to the similarity of luggage, please match your claim checks with the tags on the luggage. Please present your claim check upon request.

(20 second pause)

Correction: Flight 311, United Airlines, will *not* be leaving at this time. Flight 311 of United Airlines has been delayed. Please listen for future announcements.

(40 second pause)

Paging L. Nelson...L. Nelson, please report to the attendant at the flight information desk. There is a message for you at the flight information desk...L. Nelson.

(30 second pause)

Mexicana Airlines, Flight 15 from Mexico City, is now arriving on concourse C. People meeting passengers from Mexicana Airlines, Flight 15 should wait in the terminal and meet their parties at the end of the concourse. No one will be permitted beyond the security guards without a boarding pass...Mexicana Airlines, Flight 15 from Mexico City, now arriving on concourse C.

(40 second pause)

Will a Miss Hedley please meet your party at the flight information desk. Miss Hedley, please check with the attendant at the flight information desk.

(30 second pause)

Delta Airlines, Flight 117 to Atlanta, Orlando, and Miami, has been delayed for mechanical reasons. Please listen for further announcements. Repeating: Delta Airlines, Flight 117 has been delayed.

(15 second pause)

Alitalia Airlines, Flight 406 to New York and Rome, will depart from gate 25, concourse C. All passengers for Alitalia, Flight 406 to New York and Rome, please report to gate 25 for boarding.

(30 second pause)

Baggage from American Airlines, Flight 420, is now arriving at carousel 2. Due to the similarity of baggage, please be sure to match your claim check with the number on the luggage. Please present your claim check upon request.

(15 second pause)

Will the party paging L. Nelson repeat the page. Thank you.

(30 second pause)

Will a Mr. or Mrs. R. Solis...Mr. or Mrs. R. Solis, please call the airport police immediately...Repeat: Mr. or Mrs. R. Solis, please call the airport police.

(15 second pause)

TWA, Flight 750. TWA, Flight 750 to Chicago and Montreal, is now boarding on concourse C. Passengers on TWA Flight 750 should report to concourse C, gate 12.

(30 second pause)

C. Camden...paging C. Camden, Carlos or Carla Camden. Please go to the TWA flight information desk for a telephone message...C. Camden.

(35 second pause)

Will a Dr. or Mrs. Johnson please report to the security guard at concourse C...I repeat: will Dr. or Mrs. Johnson please report to the security guard at concourse C.

(15 second pause)

Attention please. Passengers for United Airlines, Flight 311...Passengers for United's Flight 311 to San Francisco, Flight 311 has been canceled because of technical problems. Please check with the United Airlines ticket desk in the main lobby to make new reservations. Thank you.

(25 second pause)

Paging L. Nelson. L. Nelson, your party is now waiting at the flight information desk. L. Nelson, please report to the flight information desk.

(15 second pause)

Last call for Alitalia Airlines, Flight 406. Alitalia Airlines, Flight 406 to New York and Rome is departing from gate 25.

(20 second pause)

Will someone from airport security please report to gate 20...airport security.

(15 second pause)

Will Mr. Franco Rawlings please report to the Avis service counter. Mr. Franco Rawlings, please pick up your keys at the Avis service desk.

(12 second pause)

Baggage from Mexicana Airlines, Flight 15, is now arriving at carousel 1. Due to the similarity of baggage, please be sure to match your claim checks with the tags on the luggage. Please present your claim check upon request.

(20 second pause)

Delta Airlines, Flight 117, will now depart at 2:30. Passengers on Delta Airlines, Flight 117, should note the new departure time of 2:30. For further information, please check with the Delta Airlines ticket desk.

(17 second pause)

Ladies and gentlemen, please listen to this important announcement. And *please* remain calm. People's lives may depend on your acting calmly and rationally...The Airport Authority has just received an anonymous phone call. The caller claims to have a bomb hidden in the terminal. We are asking all patrons to evacuate the building while security examines the building. *Please* do not become overly alarmed. Exit through the main lobby. Move quickly but calmly. Remember, please, this is a precaution only. Please remain calm. We repeat; please evacuate the building through the main lobby while security searches the premises for a bomb. You will receive further instructions outside the building. Move quickly but calmly. Thank you.

The Where Game

Objective:

Using pantomime, establish a WHERE in the shortest possible time.

Procedure:

The class is divided into two teams. Each team is located at different ends of the room. One volunteer from each team comes to the center of the room. The instructor shows each team volunteer a card printed with a specific "where." [Examples: (1) "In a sewing room," (2) "Inside a washing machine."] Each volunteer then rushes back to his teammates. Without speech, the student demonstrates the WHERE she has been shown. The first team to guess the WHERE earns a point. The process is repeated with new volunteers until everyone on a team has played.

Notes: Game A may be played on one day. Game B may be saved for another day. Students should expect the wheres to become more abstract as a game progresses. Also, players are reminded that they must remain *inside* a where when performing their pantomimes. They cannot establish a where from the outside. For example, suppose a card says "inside a washing machine." If a player stuffs clothes into an imaginary washing machine, you should subtract two points from his team's score. Why? He is establishing the where from OUTSIDE the washing machine. He must create the idea of being INSIDE the washing machine. (However, the other pantomime would be appropriate for "In a laundromat.")

Cut out card on dotted lines

You may want to laminate these
cards to make them more durable.

Word Charades

Objective:

To communicate, in pantomime, a series of single or compound words in the shortest time possible. Teammates must guess the exact word or phrase that is printed on each of four cards.

Procedure:

Divide the class into teams of five or six members. Two teams will compete while others observe. Team A should be sent out of the room so it cannot see or hear Team B in action. On Team B: three members should be actors and two or three should be guessers. The guessers are seated side by side. They may talk and ask questions of the actors. From behind the guessers the instructor will hold up a card from Set A. This card will display the word (or compound word) to be acted out. One actor pantomimes an action. The guessers will shout out the word or a synonym or a part of it. When students guess the word, the instructor will hold up a second word. Another actor should begin the new pantomime.

This process continues until four words have been guessed or three minutes have elapsed (whichever happens first). Then Team A is called into the room. Using the same procedure, Team A tries to guess the same four words in a shorter length of time than Team B. Repeat the contest with other teams. Use Sets B, C, D, E, and F.

Note: It is helpful to have a stopwatch and official timer when playing this game. At times an actor may get "stuck." She may be unable to communicate the word that is on display. If that happens, a second actor can "bump" the first one (or a third can bump the second one). Then the new actors can try a different approach. However, only one actor can perform at a time. A fifteen-second penalty should be imposed each time this rule is broken.

Cut out card on dotted lines

Detailed Motives

Objective:

To create several two-person scenes which hold the viewers' interest for two to four minutes as the performers develop a believable WHO, WHERE, and WHAT.

Procedure:

Actors should be assigned (or can voluntarily group themselves) into pairs. One pair acts at a time. The individual cards tell both players WHERE their scene takes place and WHO the two characters are. However, each person will read silently his/her motive (WHAT). Actor A should begin the scene alone. He/she attempts to establish the where of the scene by coming in contact with various objects or pieces of furniture in the room or area. Next, Actor B should enter the scene. He/she further helps to establish the where. At the same time he begins to establish certain facts about who the characters A and B are. The characters should speak to one another. They should establish firmly where and who they are. Afterwards their efforts should be focused on what each character wants to accomplish. They can expect that their motives will bring them into some sort of conflict.

After announcing CURTAIN! to start each scene, the instructor may side-coach Character A reminding him/her to focus on establishing a where. The instructor may also tell Character B when to enter. Further, the teacher can side-coach both performers, reminding them to stress their motives, the what. Either the performers or the instructor may call out CURTAIN! to end the scene when it seems to have runs its course.

Note: If one or two of the scenes fail to develop into an interesting conflict, try replaying the scene with both actors knowing what the other character's motive is. Or let the actors choose a new situation.

Cut out card on dotted lines

One Word Motives

Objective:

- To build on skills developed in the game DETAILED MOTIVES.
- To work more spontaneously.
- To focus more fully on the WHAT in each improvised situation.

Procedure:

Participants are divided into pairs. One pair performs at a time. All others become an audience. Member A leaves the room while Member B selects a card from the ONE WORD MOTIVE deck of cards. The audience helps Member B decide on a WHERE and a WHO appropriate for the motive he/she has chosen. Member B should decide quickly and also make up her mind who Member A is. In other words, what is the relationship between A and B in the scene they are about to play?

Member A is then called back into the room. This person is told nothing about the decisions Member B and the audience have made. The improvised scene begins with Member A on stage. Member B may request that Member A either stand or sit. Member A remains neutral until Player B enters the scene and begins talking. Even then, Member A should use vague phrases in responding to B's questions and comments.

Member B should avoid using words which directly identify the relationship between her and Player A. For example, if she is the "mother" of Member A, she should avoid calling him "son." However, she might say, "How are you feeling, David, Dear?" She could also say, "We're having hamburgers for dinner tonight, because I know you like them." Comments like these will help Member A begin to understand how he is related to Member B.

Once she has established some clues about her relationship to Member A, Member B should begin to pursue her ONE WORD MOTIVE. For example, if that motive is "to embarrass," she might say, "I was putting some laundry away in your dresser drawer today and I found some magazines that I didn't know you owned."

When he is fairly certain about who Member B is, Member A should let B know what his suspicions are with a comment like: "Mother, I don't think it's right for you to snoop in my room." Once he has discovered who he is, Member A should try to figure out B's motive and develop a motive of his own. Both players should seek to keep the scene interesting by trying to "block" their partner's motive. The instructor will call out CURTAIN! to end scenes which become confusing because of misunderstood motives. Players may also end their own scenes when they realize they have "run out of steam."

Note: If Member A misidentifies his relationship to his fellow player, Member B may follow one of three courses: (1) End the scene, because it has become too muddled. (2) Try to correct her partner's mistake with dialog: "It was sweet of you to call me 'Grandmother,' David, but you know full well that I'm your mother. Remember, Grandmother ended her visit here last Sunday." (3) Accept "the misidentification and play the remainder of the scene in the new role that Member A has created for her.

Cut out card on dotted lines

Adding Characters and Shifting Motives

Objective:

- To continue to develop scene building techniques involving WHERE, WHO, and WHAT.

- To adapt characterizations as new players and information are added to a scene.

Procedure:

Divide the class into teams of six players. One team performs at a time. The other teams become an audience. The six performers will be given individual cards explaining WHERE they are, WHO they are, and WHAT their character wants. They should not look at each other's cards or preplan the scene in any way. Players will enter the scene singly or in pairs as coached by the instructor.

Character A enters first, then B, then C, etc. Performer A begins the scene by establishing WHERE the action takes place. She strongly suggests WHO she is. Her actions may also suggest WHAT motives are strongest in her mind at the moment the scene begins. When Performer B enters the scene, he should use dialog and actions to establish how he knows or is related to Character A. Character B also has a WHAT. He may urge Character A to help him with his need. Performer A should accept the new information the second character introduces. She may ask questions and either join Character B in pursuing a new motive or ignore his needs. Performer B must also adapt to information that Performer A adds or reveals while creating dialog.

As the next four characters enter, further adaptation and acceptance of new information will be necessary. Identity cards for Performers C, D, and E explain who they are and what their motives are. The new information they introduce will usually influence the motives of everyone already on stage. Performer F may choose his own who and what. He has the responsibility of trying to end the scene. All six players should work toward bringing the improvisation to a logical conclusion shortly after Performer F's entrance. For additional suggestions about this exercise, see page 21 of the *Student Handbook* and page 41 of the *Teacher's Guide*.

Cut out card on dotted lines

Christmas Rush

Objective:

- To remain "in character."

- To keep the scene interesting.

- To "give" and to "take" during a scene.

- To avoid dividing an audience's focus of attention.

Procedure:

Assign eleven or twelve volunteers a role by handing them a card. Explain that the scene is a local post office at Christmas time. Eight characters will be on stage when the scene begins. Characters #5, #10, #11, and #12 will enter as it develops. Their cards explain when they should come into the scene. One possible arrangement of furniture to suggest a post office interior is diagramed on page 49 of the *Teacher's Guide*. The instructor and performers may alter this plan. However, it is important that all participants know the layout of the post office before the improvisation begins.

When the instructor signals the start of the scene, Character #1 and Character #6 should capture the initial focus with their improvised dialog. After that, it is difficult to predict how the scene will or should progress. All performers should practice their skills of "giving" and "taking" a scene. Each student will act out his/her character's need for being at the post office. After doing so, some actors may decide that logically their character should leave the scene and not return. This is a complex improvisation. Therefore, actors should not feel it is necessary to unify or resolve all conflicts at the end of the exercise. For more suggestions about ways to maintain focus during this exercise, consult the *Student Handbook* (page 24) and the *Teacher's Guide* (page 47).

Cut out card on dotted lines

International Airport

Objective:

- To develop the skills of "giving" and "taking" a scene while remaining in character.

- To aid an audience in knowing where to focus its attention.

Procedure:

Twelve to sixteen people participate in this scene. It is set in the passenger waiting area of an international airport. The instructor hands out an appropriate number of "identities" to participants. They must then fill out a FACT SHEET before the scene begins. Two or three additional volunteers may be assigned roles such as flight information desk attendant, security guard, and/or flight dispatcher. One possible arrangement for the location of furniture and exits in the scene is diagramed on page 53 of the *Teacher's Guide*. The diagram assumes that the players will be working on a proscenium stage. It is important that all participants know the layout of the airport before the improvisation begins.

Note: The scene should be played without any attempt to create a central dramatic conflict. Individual characters may discover some minor conflicts between themselves and another character in the scene. But the group should focus on establishing a collection of WHOs in a given WHERE. They should focus less on developing a story line. Ultimately, the minor conflicts will keep the scene interesting.

Cut out card on dotted lines

You may want to laminate these cards to make them more durable.

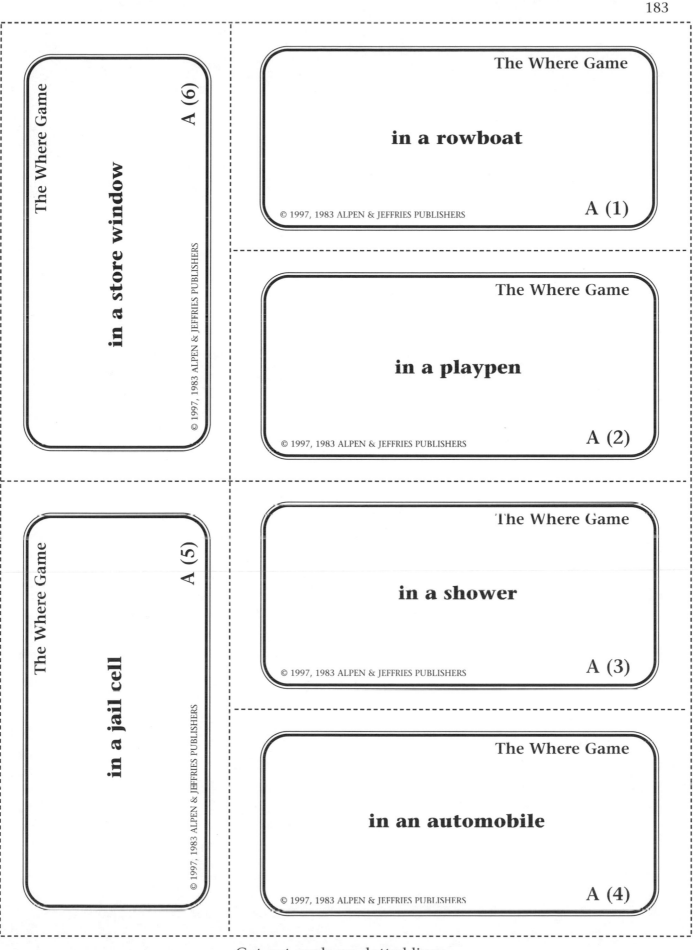

The Where Game

A (6)

in a store window

© 1997, 1983 ALPEN & JEFFRIES PUBLISHERS

The Where Game

in a rowboat

© 1997, 1983 ALPEN & JEFFRIES PUBLISHERS

A (1)

The Where Game

in a playpen

© 1997, 1983 ALPEN & JEFFRIES PUBLISHERS

A (2)

The Where Game

A (5)

in a jail cell

© 1997, 1983 ALPEN & JEFFRIES PUBLISHERS

The Where Game

in a shower

© 1997, 1983 ALPEN & JEFFRIES PUBLISHERS

A (3)

The Where Game

in an automobile

© 1997, 1983 ALPEN & JEFFRIES PUBLISHERS

A (4)

Cut out cards on dotted lines

The Where Game

A (12)

in a television set

© 1997, 1983 ALPEN & JEFFRIES PUBLISHERS

The Where Game

in a barber shop

© 1997, 1983 ALPEN & JEFFRIES PUBLISHERS

A (7)

The Where Game

in a haunted house

© 1997, 1983 ALPEN & JEFFRIES PUBLISHERS

A (8)

The Where Game

A (11)

in a shoe

© 1997, 1983 ALPEN & JEFFRIES PUBLISHERS

The Where Game

in a submarine

© 1997, 1983 ALPEN & JEFFRIES PUBLISHERS

A (9)

The Where Game

in a beehive

© 1997, 1983 ALPEN & JEFFRIES PUBLISHERS

A (10)

Cut out cards on dotted lines

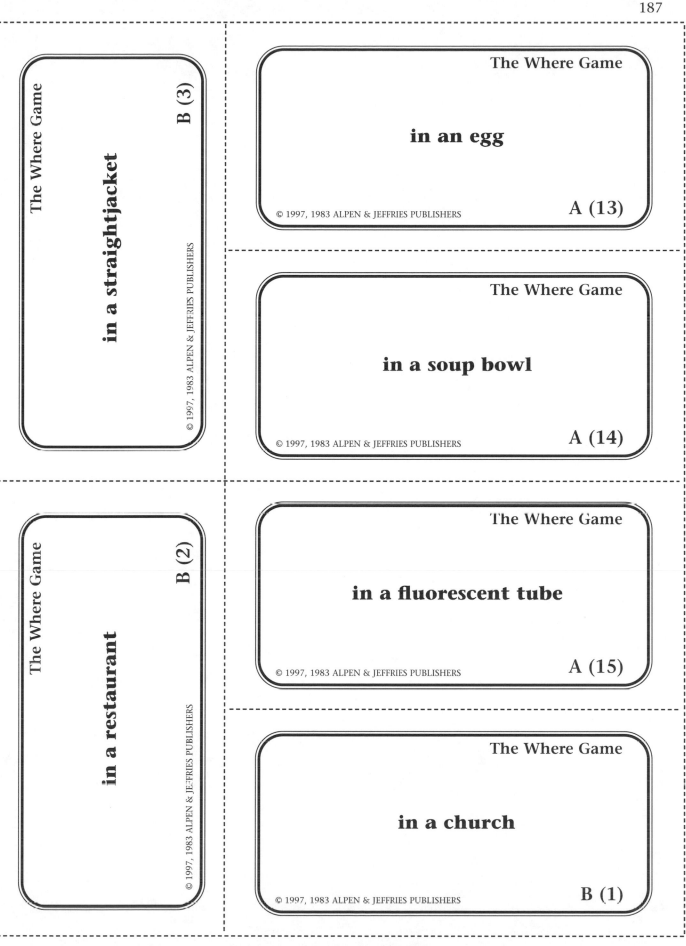

The Where Game

in a straightjacket

B (3)

© 1997, 1983 ALPEN & JEFFRIES PUBLISHERS

The Where Game

in a restaurant

B (2)

© 1997, 1983 ALPEN & JEFFRIES PUBLISHERS

The Where Game

in an egg

© 1997, 1983 ALPEN & JEFFRIES PUBLISHERS

A (13)

The Where Game

in a soup bowl

© 1997, 1983 ALPEN & JEFFRIES PUBLISHERS

A (14)

The Where Game

in a fluorescent tube

© 1997, 1983 ALPEN & JEFFRIES PUBLISHERS

A (15)

The Where Game

in a church

© 1997, 1983 ALPEN & JEFFRIES PUBLISHERS

B (1)

Cut out cards on dotted lines

The Where Game

B (9)

in a Broadway chorus line

© 1997, 1983 ALPEN & JEFFRIES PUBLISHERS

The Where Game

in a swimming pool

B (4)

© 1997, 1983 ALPEN & JEFFRIES PUBLISHERS

The Where Game

in an operating room

B (5)

© 1997, 1983 ALPEN & JEFFRIES PUBLISHERS

The Where Game

B (8)

in a hot air balloon

© 1997, 1983 ALPEN & JEFFRIES PUBLISHERS

The Where Game

in a classroom

B (6)

© 1997, 1983 ALPEN & JEFFRIES PUBLISHERS

The Where Game

in an art gallery

B (7)

© 1997, 1983 ALPEN & JEFFRIES PUBLISHERS

Cut out cards on dotted lines

The Where Game

B (15)

in a tube of
toothpaste

© 1997, 1983 ALPEN & JEFFRIES PUBLISHERS

The Where Game

in a maze

© 1997, 1983 ALPEN & JEFFRIES PUBLISHERS

B (10)

The Where Game

in a trash can

© 1997, 1983 ALPEN & JEFFRIES PUBLISHERS

B (11)

The Where Game

B (14)

in a grandfather
clock

© 1997, 1983 ALPEN & JEFFRIES PUBLISHERS

The Where Game

in a fish bowl

© 1997, 1983 ALPEN & JEFFRIES PUBLISHERS

B (12)

The Where Game

in a mother's womb

© 1997, 1983 ALPEN & JEFFRIES PUBLISHERS

B (13)

Cut out cards on dotted lines

Word Charades

menu

A (1)

Word Charades

cemetery

A (2)

Word Charades

ham

A (3)

Word Charades

horoscope

A (4)

Word Charades

B (2)

peanut butter

Word Charades

B (1)

rocking chair

Cut out cards on dotted lines

Word Charades

windmill

B (3)

Word Charades

sister

B (4)

Word Charades

calendar

C (1)

Word Charades

pirate

C (2)

Word Charades

C (4)

fudge

Word Charades

C (3)

trout

Cut out cards on dotted lines

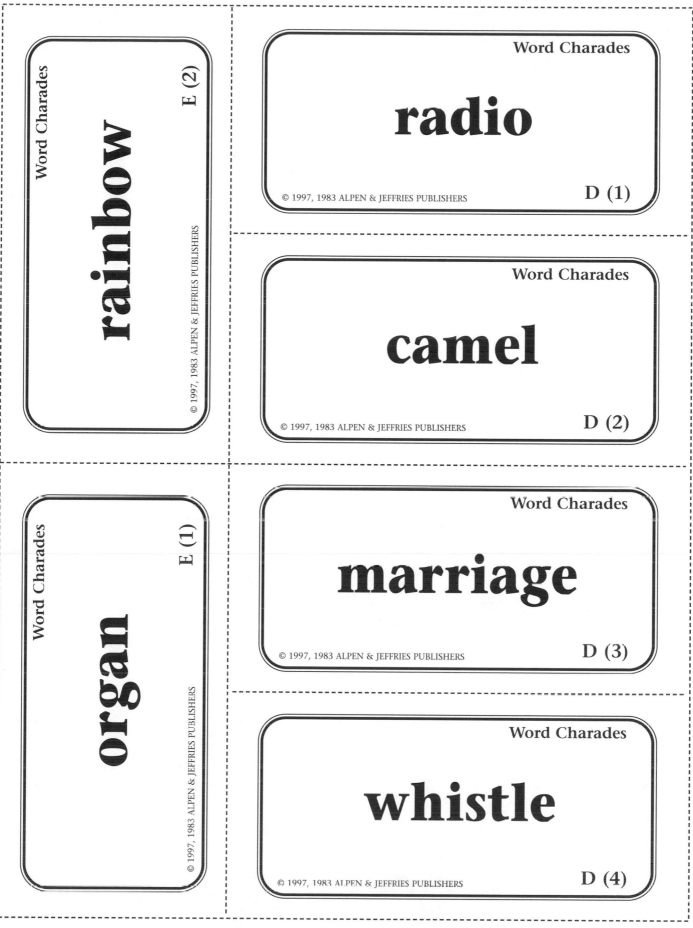

Word Charades

rainbow

E (2)

Word Charades

radio

D (1)

Word Charades

camel

D (2)

Word Charades

organ

E (1)

Word Charades

marriage

D (3)

Word Charades

whistle

D (4)

Cut out cards on dotted lines

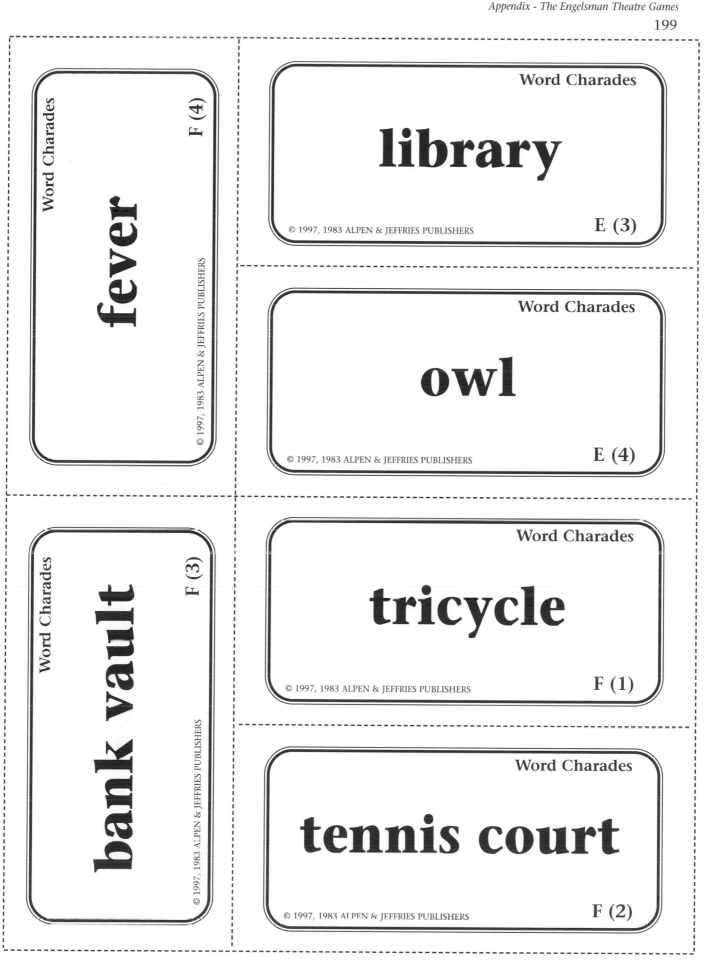

Word Charades

library

© 1997, 1983 ALPEN & JEFFRIES PUBLISHERS

E (3)

Word Charades

owl

© 1997, 1983 ALPEN & JEFFRIES PUBLISHERS

E (4)

Word Charades

tricycle

© 1997, 1983 ALPEN & JEFFRIES PUBLISHERS

F (1)

Word Charades

tennis court

© 1997, 1983 ALPEN & JEFFRIES PUBLISHERS

F (2)

Word Charades

F (4)

fever

© 1997, 1983 ALPEN & JEFFRIES PUBLISHERS

Word Charades

F (3)

bank vault

© 1997, 1983 ALPEN & JEFFRIES PUBLISHERS

Cut out cards on dotted lines

Cut out cards on dotted lines

Detailed Motives

Character 1A

Where:
Office of a large business firm.

Who:
You are a secretary (male or female).
Character B is a young staff worker of the opposite sex.

What:
You want to work your way up in the firm. You would like to have the young staff person's job. Therefore, you want to learn as much as you can about his/her job. You particularly want to learn where he/she may be cutting corners or *not* working efficiently.

Detailed Motives

Character 1B

Where:
Office of a large business firm.

Who:
You are a young staff person in the office.
Character A is a secretary of the opposite sex.

What:
You wish to have a date with the secretary. But before asking this person out, you want to know if he/she is dating someone, where the person lives (and with whom), and the interests of this person.

Detailed Motives

Character 2A

Where:
Apartment living room.

Who:
You are a female who lives in the apartment.
Character B is an appliance repairman.

What:
You have murdered your husband. His body parts are hidden in the oven. You do not want the repairman in the kitchen. You did not call the repairman. You want him to leave.

Cut out cards on dotted lines

Cut out cards on dotted lines

Detailed Motives

Character 2B

Who:

You are an appliance repairman. *Character A is a woman.*

Where:

Apartment living room.

What:

You have a work order to repair a broken stove. It has not worked for several weeks. The apartment manager put in a rush repair order. Your boss told you not to leave the apartment until this stove is repaired. The apartment manager is insistent that the stove be repaired today.

© 1997, 1983 ALPEN & JEFFRIES PUBLISHERS

Detailed Motives

Character 3A

Who:

You are an attractive single person wearing a skimpy bathing suit. *Character B is a native of the city selling necklaces. Character B is of the opposite sex.*

Where:

A beach at a resort hotel.

What:

You do not want to pay the prices the salesperson is asking. However, talking to the salesperson does allow you to stand up and be observed by others.

© 1997, 1983 ALPEN & JEFFRIES PUBLISHERS

Detailed Motives

Character 3B

Who:

You are a native of the city trying to sell necklaces made of coral or shells. *Character A is an attractive person of the opposite sex in a bathing suit.*

Where:

A beach at a resort hotel.

What:

You want to sell your merchandise at a good price. You want to make a sale.

© 1997, 1983 ALPEN & JEFFRIES PUBLISHERS

Cut out cards on dotted lines

Character 4A

Detailed Motives

Where:

A tenth reunion party.

Who:

You are a single female member of the reunion class. *Character B is a former classmate and a former boyfriend.*

What:

Your former classmate has recently been divorced. You are wearing an expensive diamond necklace that you bought at a local jewelry store. You also are wearing a bracelet that you purchased from his ex-wife. You do not want him to notice the bracelet. However, you do not want to appear rude or unfriendly.

Character 4B

Detailed Motives

Where:

A tenth reunion party.

Who:

You are a recently divorced male member of the reunion class. *Character A is an attractive former girl-friend. She is wearing an expensive looking diamond* necklace.

What:

You are a burglar. Of course, you do not want to reveal that fact to Character A. However, you would like to learn more about the necklace she is wearing, where she lives, and who else lives with her. You need this information to set up your next robbery at her house!

Character 5A

Detailed Motives

Where:

In line waiting to get into a movie theatre.

Who:

You are a movie star. *Character B is your ex-spouse whom you divorced three years ago.*

What:

You do not mind seeing your ex-spouse. But you do not want to be recognized by other people waiting in line. They might ask you for your auto-graph. You want to see the movie.

Cut out cards on dotted lines

Character 5B

Where:

In line waiting to get into a movie theatre.

Who:

You are the ex-spouse of Character A. You have been divorced for three years. *Character A is a movie star.*

What:

This is a chance meeting. You would like to rekindle your old friendship with your ex-spouse.

Character 6A

Where:

A bus stop late at night.

Who:

You are a teenage girl. *Character B is a friendly young man in his early twenties.*

What:

Because this is a strange city neighborhood, you are frightened and would like the young man to stay until your bus arrives.

Character 6B

Where:

A bus stop late at night.

Who:

You are a man in your early twenties. *Character A is a teenage girl.*

What:

A block from the bus stop is a gas station that is open. You hope to find a rest room there. You need to find a bathroom soon. However, you do not want to reveal your problem to the girl.

Cut out cards on dotted lines

Character 7A

Detailed Motives

Where:

The lobby of a resort hotel in a small town.

Who:

You are a female guest at the hotel. *Character B is another guest who is approximately your age and who has just arrived.*

What:

Your stay so far has been boring and you want to strike up a "meaningful relationship" with this new guest.

Character 7B

Detailed Motives

Where:

The lobby of a resort hotel in a small town.

Who:

You are a male Secret Service agent posing as a guest. *Character A is another hotel guest approximately your age.*

What:

You want to keep your true identity a secret and not arouse curiosity as you "case the joint" as a possible place for a presidential summit meeting next month.

Character 8A

Detailed Motives

Where:

A public library.

Who:

You are a librarian. *Character B is a person who was your teacher ten years ago.*

What:

Because you cannot recall your teacher's name, you want to keep him/her in conversation hoping the name will be revealed in your conversation.

Cut out cards on dotted lines

Detailed Motives

Character 8B

Where:

A public library.

Who:

You are a teacher. *Character A is a librarian who was your former student ten years ago.*

What:

You want to return a long overdue book back onto the library shelves. You want to return this book without being detected or observed.

© 1997, 1983 ALPEN & JEFFRIES PUBLISHERS

Detailed Motives

Character 9A

Where:

A fashionable jewelry store

Who:

You are a clerk in the store. *Character B is a nicely dressed customer.*

What:

You want to scratch an itch that is in an embarrassing place. The itch should become more irritating as the scene progresses. The urge to itch should become more critical.

© 1997, 1983 ALPEN & JEFFRIES PUBLISHERS

Detailed Motives

Character 9B

Where:

A fashionable jewelry store

Who:

You are a customer entering the store. *Character A is a dignified clerk.*

What:

You are pretending that you want to buy a piece of jewelry. You are wasting time in the store because an unattractive "blind date" is waiting to meet you in front of the store. You want to avoid this meeting.

© 1997, 1983 ALPEN & JEFFRIES PUBLISHERS

Cut out cards on dotted lines

Detailed Motives

Character 10A

Where:

A rustic cabin in a wooded area.

Who:

You are a novelist, the owner of the cabin. *Character B is a stranger who has wandered onto your property.*

What:

You want to be alone so you can concentrate on your writing.

Detailed Motives

Character 10B

Where:

A rustic cabin in a wooded area.

Who:

You are an escaped convict. *Character A is the owner of the cabin.*

What:

Character A does *not* know that you are an escaped convict. Character A's card identifies you as a "stranger." You want a place to hide. You want to avoid being identified.

Detailed Motives

Character 11A

Where:

A restaurant.

Who:

You are a customer ordering food at the restaurant. *Character B is a waiter or waitress.*

What:

You recognize the waiter or waitress as someone who once was your employer several years ago. You want to order and eat your meal without being recognized.

Cut out cards on dotted lines

Cut out cards on dotted lines

Character 11B

Where:
A restaurant.

Who:
You are a waiter or waitress. *Character A is a customer.*

What:
You want to hurry the customer's selection. This will be your last customer of the evening. If you remain nearby, the customer might get the message.

Character 12A

Where:
On board a commercial airliner in flight.

Who:
You are a passenger seated next to a child. *Character B is an airline steward or stewardess in the aisle.*

What:
The child next to you is sick and looks as if he will throw up at any moment. You want the stewardess to offer some help and assistance to the child.

Character 12B

Where:
On board a commercial airliner in flight.

Who:
You are an airline steward or stewardess. *Character A is a passenger seated next to a child.*

What:
The pilot has received notice of a phoned-in bomb threat. Your job is to surreptitiously search for a bomb without alarming passengers.

Cut out cards on dotted lines

Detailed Motives

Character 13A

Who:

You are a burglar's accomplice. *Character B is a rookie cop.*

Where:

Outside a home in a residential area at night.

What:

You want to appear to be "merely" out for a breath of fresh air. You want to get the rookie cop to move on.

© 1997, 1983 ALPEN & JEFFRIES PUBLISHERS

Detailed Motives

Character 13B

Who:

You are a rookie cop. *Character A is a citizen out for an evening stroll.*

Where:

Outside a home in a residential area at night.

What:

You want to strike up a conversation and keep it going. You are lonely and just a little bit frightened.

© 1997, 1983 ALPEN & JEFFRIES PUBLISHERS

Detailed Motives

Character 14A

Who:

You are a clerk at the store. *Character B is an underage customer with a phony ID.*

Where:

A liquor store.

What:

You want to stall the customer. There is a hold-up man in the back room who has allowed you to come and wait on this customer.

© 1997, 1983 ALPEN & JEFFRIES PUBLISHERS

Cut out cards on dotted lines

Character 14B

Where:
A liquor store.

Who:
You are an underage customer with a phony ID card. *Character A is the clerk at the store.*

What:
You want to purchase two six packs of beer and a bottle of whiskey. You want the clerk to think that you are legal age.

© 1997, 1983 ALPEN & JEFFRIES PUBLISHERS

Character 15A

Where:
The waiting room of a dentist's office.

Who:
You are a patient and a celebrated novelist. *Character B is another patient.*

What:
The dentist has given you a large dose of Novocaine and it has made your mouth numb. You want *not* to talk because you know your speech will be slurred.

© 1997, 1983 ALPEN & JEFFRIES PUBLISHERS

Character 15B

Where:
The waiting room of a dentist's office.

Who:
You are a patient. *Character A is also a patient. He/she is a celebrated novelist whom you recognize from his/her picture.*

What:
As an amateur writer, you would like to start a conversation with the novelist. You would like the novelist to read one of your manuscripts.

© 1997, 1983 ALPEN & JEFFRIES PUBLISHERS

Cut out cards on dotted lines

Detailed Motives

Character 16A

Who:

You are a shoplifter. *Character B is a lost child.*

Where:

A department store.

What:

Having already pocketed several small items, you want to get out of the store as inconspicuously as possible.

Detailed Motives

Character 16B

Who:

You are a lost child. *Character A is a shoplifter.*

Where:

A department store.

What:

You cannot find your "mommy." You recognize Character A as an acquaintance of your "mommy." You want Character A to help you find your "mommy."

Detailed Motives

Character 17A

Who:

You are a museum guard. *Character B is a teenager visiting the museum.*

Where:

A room in a museum containing a mummy's tomb.

What:

You have placed a sandwich in the mummy's tomb. You want to prevent the teenage viewer from discovering it.

Cut out cards on dotted lines

Detailed Motives

Character 17B

Where:

A room in a museum containing a mummy's tomb.

Who:

You are a museum visitor in your teens. *Character A is a museum guard.*

What:

Your friends have dared you to touch the mummy's wrapped body. You want to distract the guard so you can meet their dare.

Detailed Motives

Character 18A

Where:

An empty subway car at 1:00 a.m.

Who:

You are a rider reading a newspaper. *Character B is a rider with a suitcase.*

What:

Afraid of germs, you want to keep some distance between yourself and the other passenger. You also want to read your newspaper.

Detailed Motives

Character 18B

Where:

An empty subway car at 1:00 a.m.

Who:

You are a rider with a suitcase. *Character A is a rider reading a newspaper.*

What:

You are a traveler new to the city. You are not sure that you are on the right train. Character A is reading a newspaper. On the back of the newspaper is a headline which reads: SUBWAY CRIME WAVE. You would like to read the article.

Cut out cards on dotted lines

Detailed Motives

Character 19A

Where:

The head table at a testimonial dinner.

Who:

You are the featured speaker. *Character B, seated next to you, is one of the organizers of the dinner.*

What:

You have forgotten the copy of the speech you are giving at the dinner. You need to make some notes for your speech. However, you do not wish to be rude to Character B.

© 1997, 1983 ALPEN & JEFFRIES PUBLISHERS

Detailed Motives

Character 19B

Where:

The head table at a testimonial dinner.

Who:

You are one of the hosts who has planned and organized the dinner. *Character A, seated next to you, is the featured speaker.*

What:

Character A is known to be shy. You want to put him/her at ease. You plan to ask questions or entertain him/her with amusing small talk.

© 1997, 1983 ALPEN & JEFFRIES PUBLISHERS

Detailed Motives

Character 20A

Where:

The aisles of a grocery store.

Who:

You are a grocery clerk. You want to earn extra money. You have taken a second job at the grocery store as their night janitor. This particular evening you brought your own two mops and two large buckets to use. You plan to use them when you mop the floors tonight. *Character B is the store manager waiting to lock the store.*

What:

In addition to mops, the buckets now contain two large cuts of beef that you stole from the meat department's freezer. The mops cover the wrapped packages. After you mop the floors, you want to leave the store without anyone noticing the packages under the mops.

© 1997, 1983 ALPEN & JEFFRIES PUBLISHERS

Character 20B

Where:

The aisles of a grocery store.

Detailed Motives

Who:

You are the store manager waiting to lock the store after Character A completes mopping the aisles. *Character A is a grocery clerk who wants to earn extra money as the night janitor. This particular evening Character A is using his own two mops and two buckets.*

What:

Two aisles in the store still look dirty. You want the janitor/clerk to mop them again with his wet mops. Since you want to go home, offer to mop one of the two remaining aisles. Knowing that the clerk works long hours, you want to help him.

Cut out card on dotted lines

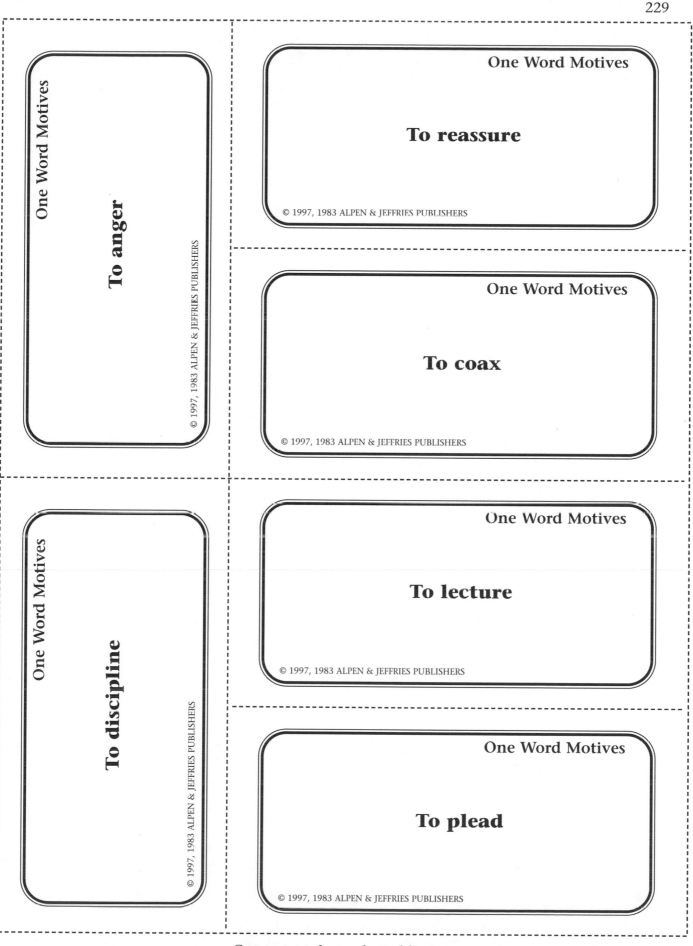

One Word Motives

To anger

One Word Motives

To reassure

One Word Motives

To coax

One Word Motives

To discipline

One Word Motives

To lecture

One Word Motives

To plead

Cut out cards on dotted lines

One Word Motives

To ignore

One Word Motives

To persuade

One Word Motives

To distract

One Word Motives

To learn the truth

One Word Motives

To fluster

One Word Motives

To flatter

Cut out cards on dotted lines

One Word Motives

To reject

One Word Motives

To humiliate

One Word Motives

To amuse

One Word Motives

To get your companion to leave

One Word Motives

To teach

One Word Motives

To tease

Cut out cards on dotted lines

One Word Motives

To confuse

This behavior may be the character's *conscious* motive or it may merely be the *effect* of his/her *behavior*.

One Word Motives

To stall

One Word Motives

To make your companion laugh

One Word Motives

To bore

This behavior may be the character's *conscious* motive or it may merely be the *effect* of his/her behavior.

One Word Motives

To follow

One Word Motives

To question

Cut out cards on dotted lines

One Word Motives

To upset

This behavior may be the character's *conscious* motive or it may merely be the *effect* of his/her behavior.

© 1997, 1983 ALPEN & JEFFRIES PUBLISHERS

One Word Motives

To excite

This behavior may be the character's *conscious* motive or it may merely be the *effect* of his/her behavior.

© 1997, 1983 ALPEN & JEFFRIES PUBLISHERS

One Word Motives

To make jealous

This behavior may be the character's *conscious* motive or it may merely be the *effect* of his/her behavior.

© 1997, 1983 ALPEN & JEFFRIES PUBLISHERS

One Word Motives

To amaze or astound

This behavior may be the character's *conscious* motive or it may merely be the *effect* of his/her behavior.

© 1997, 1983 ALPEN & JEFFRIES PUBLISHERS

One Word Motives

To irritate

This behavior may be the character's *conscious* motive or it may merely be the *effect* of his/her behavior.

© 1997, 1983 ALPEN & JEFFRIES PUBLISHERS

One Word Motives

To frighten

This behavior may be the character's *conscious* motive or it may merely be the *effect* of his\her behavior.

© 1997, 1983 ALPEN & JEFFRIES PUBLISHERS

Situation #1

Adding Characters and Shifting Motives

Character A
female

Where:
The family kitchen.

Who:
You are a tired businesswoman arriving home after a hard day's work.

What:
You want to relax and unwind.

Situation #1

Adding Characters and Shifting Motives

Character B
male

Where:
The family kitchen.

Who:
You are Character A's husband, an insurance salesman. You have been married for fourteen years.

What:
You are late getting home from work. More importantly, there is a testimonial dinner for your boss tonight. You must *quickly* change into formal clothes and go downtown. You want your wife, who has forgotten about the dinner, to get dressed as quickly as possible.

Situation #1

Adding Characters Shifting Motives

Character C
female

Where:
The family kitchen.

Who:
You are Character A's mother.

What:
You and your husband of thirty-nine years have had a quarrel. There have been many quarrels recently. You are considering getting a divorce. You want to stay at your daughter's place for a few days. You want her to listen to your troubles, *now*.

Cut out cards on dotted lines

Cut out cards on dotted lines

Situation #1

Adding Characters and Shifting Motives

Character D
male or female

Who:
You are the neighbor of Characters A and B. You are *not* close friends.

Where:
The family kitchen.

What:
Your daughter's red bicycle has been stolen. Someone else in the neighborhood said he saw Character A and Character B's son (or daughter) riding a red bike. You want to talk to their child. You also want to look in their basement or garage to see if the bike is there.

© 1997, 1983 ALPEN & JEFFRIES PUBLISHERS

Situation #1

Adding Characters and Shifting Motives

Character E
male or female

Who:
You are a police officer.

Where:
The family kitchen.

What:
There has been an accident at an intersection, a block away. A young boy (or girl) riding a red bike was hit by a car. Someone said he thought the child lived at this address. You want Characters A and B to come to the hospital to identify the unconscious child.

© 1997, 1983 ALPEN & JEFFRIES PUBLISHERS

Situation #1

Adding Characters and Shifting Motives

Character F
male or female

Who:
You may choose your own identity.

Where:
The family kitchen.

What:
Who you are or what new information you bring to the scene should resolve some of the major conflicts in this scene. This character's information should help everyone on stage bring the scene to a close.

© 1997, 1983 ALPEN & JEFFRIES PUBLISHERS

Cut out cards on dotted lines

Adding Characters and Shifting Motives

Situation #2

Character A
male or female

Where:

A drugstore in a city, five minutes before closing time.

Who:

You are a druggist, age forty-five. You own the drugstore. You are the only person on duty.

What:

You want to close the drugstore, count the money from the cash register, and go home.

© 1997, 1983 ALPEN & JEFFRIES PUBLISHERS

Adding Characters and Shifting Motives

Situation #2

Character B
male or female

Where:

A drugstore in a city, five minutes before closing time.

Who:

You are a regular customer. The druggist knows your name.

What:

Your child is sick. The pediatrician has not yet returned your telephone call. You want the druggist to refill an old prescription. This particular prescription is labeled NOT REFILLABLE. Legally, the pediatrician needs to authorize a new prescription for your child.

© 1997, 1983 ALPEN & JEFFRIES PUBLISHERS

Adding Characters and Shifting Motives

Situation #2

Character C
male or female

Where:

A drugstore in a city, five minutes before closing time.

Who:

You are an ex-convict who has served time for robbery. You are presently on parole.

What:

The streets looked empty outside. You have not eaten in several days. You want to get enough money from the robbery to buy a good meal.

© 1997, 1983 ALPEN & JEFFRIES PUBLISHERS

Cut out cards on dotted lines

Adding Characters and Shifting Motives

Situation #2

Character D
male or female

Where:

A drugstore in a city, five minutes before closing time.

Who:

You are Character C's parole officer.

What:

You have suspected that Character C has been weakening in his/her decision to go "straight." You have been following Character C. You want to convince Character C not to commit the robbery.

© 1997, 1983 ALPEN & JEFFRIES PUBLISHERS

Adding Characters and Shifting Motives

Situation #2

Character E
male or female

Where:

A drugstore in a city, five minutes before closing time.

(Enter this scene through a different "door" than the one that the other characters have been using.)

Who:

You are the druggist's young son or daughter.

What:

You have been waiting in a back room for your dad (or mom) to close the store. You have been playing with a poisonous pet snake. The poisonous snake has escaped. You want to find it.

© 1997, 1983 ALPEN & JEFFRIES PUBLISHERS

Adding Characters and Shifting Motives

Situation #2

Character F
male or female

Where:

A drugstore in a city, five minutes before closing time.

Who:

You may choose your own identity.

What:

Who you are or any new information you bring to this scene should resolve some of the major conflicts. This character's information should help everyone on stage bring the scene to a close.

© 1997, 1983 ALPEN & JEFFRIES PUBLISHERS

Cut out cards on dotted lines

Cut out cards on dotted lines

Adding Characters and Shifting Motives

Situation #3

Character A
male

Where:
The city garbage dump in the early evening.

Who:
You are a middle-aged homeowner.

What:
The city-wide garbage strike is now in its second week. You are carrying a bag of garbage. You also have a carload of garbage (off-stage) that you want to leave at the dump.

© 1997, 1983 ALPEN & JEFFRIES PUBLISHERS

Adding Characters and Shifting Motives

Situation #3

Character B
male

Where:
The city garbage dump in the early evening.

Who:
You are a striking garbage collector. You are twenty-five years old.

What:
Your union has assigned you to patrol the garbage dump. You want to persuade citizens *not* to bring their garbage out to the dump. The pile up of trash in the city improves the union's bargaining power.

© 1997, 1983 ALPEN & JEFFRIES PUBLISHERS

Adding Characters and Shifting Motives

Situation #3

Character C
female

Where:
The city garbage dump in the early evening.

Who:
You are the garbage collector's wife. You arrive on the scene at the same time as Character D.

What:
You want your husband to come home. The radio says that the National Guard has been called. Union leaders have threatened violence. You do not want your spouse to get hurt.

© 1997, 1983 ALPEN & JEFFRIES PUBLISHERS

Cut out cards on dotted lines

Adding Characters and Shifting Motives

Situation #3

Character D
male or female

Where:

The city garbage dump in the early evening.

Who:

You are the garbage collector's four-year-old child. You arrive on the scene at the same time as Character C.

What:

You want your daddy to come home. He has been away a great deal. He promised that he would fix your rocking horse. You want your "horsie" fixed *now.*

© 1997, 1983 ALPEN & JEFFRIES PUBLISHERS

Adding Characters and Shifting Motives

Situation #3

Character E
female

Where:

The city garbage dump in the early evening.

Who:

You are Character A's wife.

What:

Your diamond ring is missing. You remember taking it off in the kitchen. You remember placing it on the counter near the garbage. You want to search through all of the garbage that your husband has brought to the dump.

© 1997, 1983 ALPEN & JEFFRIES PUBLISHERS

Adding Characters and Shifting Motives

Situation #3

Character F
male or female

Where:

The city garbage dump in the early evening.

Who:

You may choose your own identity.

What:

Who you are or the new information you bring to the scene should resolve some of the major conflicts. Character F's information will help everyone on stage bring the scene to a close.

© 1997, 1983 ALPEN & JEFFRIES PUBLISHERS

Cut out cards on dotted lines

Cut out cards on dotted lines

Situation #4

Adding Characters and Shifting Motives

Character A
male

Who:
You are married. Both your washer and dryer are broken. You have only one hour to do the laundry. You and your wife need clean clothes to wear to work.

Where:
A laundromat at 6:00 a.m.

What:
You want to wash some clothes. You cannot wait until your machines are repaired. You need clean clothes by 7:00 a.m.

Situation #4

Adding Characters and Shifting Motives

Character B
male or female

Who:
You are a TV announcer who is on assignment for a soap commercial.

Where:
A laundromat at 6:00 a.m.

What:
You want the man to test your product, "Awash!" and compare it to his normal laundry detergent.

Situation #4

Adding Characters and Shifting Motives

Character C
male or female

Who:
You are an advertising executive. You are supervising the filming of the commercial. A camera technician accompanies you. You are filming this commercial secretly behind a wall.

Where:
A laundromat at 6:00 a.m.

What:
OPTION #1: (Use OPTION #1: if Character A agrees to participate in the commercial.) The television camera did not record the scene. You want Character A and Character B to recreate the scene they have just completed.

Cut out cards on dotted lines

Adding Characters and Shifting Motives

Situation #4

Character C
male or female

Where:

A laundromat at 6:00 a.m.

© 1997, 1983 ALPEN & JEFFRIES PUBLISHERS

Who:

You are an advertising executive. You are supervising the filming of the commercial. A camera technician accompanies you. You are filming this commercial secretly behind a wall.

What:

OPTION #2: *(Use OPTION #2: if Character A does not want to participate in the commercial.)* You want to convince Character A that he is the perfect subject for this commercial. You want him to make the commercial. Offer him money if necessary.

Adding Characters and Shifting Motives

Situation #4

Character D
male or female

Where:

A laundromat at 6:00 a.m.

© 1997, 1983 ALPEN & JEFFRIES PUBLISHERS

Who:

You are a customer. You arrive with dirty laundry.

What:

You quickly realize that the people at this laundromat are filming a commercial. You want to be in the commercial. In fact, you want the announcer to use you *instead* of Character A.

Adding Characters and Shifting Motives

Situation #4

Character E
female

Where:

A laundromat at 6:00 a.m.

© 1997, 1983 ALPEN & JEFFRIES PUBLISHERS

Who:

You are the wife of Character A. You are dressed strangely.

What:

All of your clothes are dirty. You need your blouse and underwear. You want them as soon as possible. You do not understand why your husband is delayed. You need to go to work.

Cut out cards on dotted lines

Adding Characters and Shifting Motives

Situation #4

Character F
male or female

Where:

A laundromat at 6:00 a.m.

Who:
You may choose your own identity.

What:
Who you are or the new information you bring to this scene resolves some of the major conflicts. This character's information helps everyone on stage bring the scene to a close.

Cut out card on dotted lines

Christmas Rush

Character 1

Where:

The Post Office — When the scene begins, you are behind the postal counter. You call out, "Number 73." That person will be your next customer.

Who:

You are one of three postal clerks serving customers at the counter. You are an irritable person but you are knowledgeable and efficient.

What:

Clerk #2 is lazy. You want this clerk to do his/her job thoroughly and effectively. You just want Clerk #2 to serve customers. Clerk #3 is new and inexperienced. You want Clerk #3 to stop asking questions. You want Clerk #3 to learn the answers by himself.

© 1997, 1983 ALPEN & JEFFRIES PUBLISHERS

Christmas Rush

Character 2

Where:

The Post Office — When the scene begins, you are behind the postal counter. You are operating the postage meter and placing labels on packages.

Who:

You are one of three postal clerks serving customers at the counter. You are slow moving and good at finding busy work to avoid the job of serving customers.

What:

You want the other two clerks to handle most of the customers. You enjoy making these late shoppers and mailers wait. You say to yourself, "They should have mailed their packages earlier."

© 1997, 1983 ALPEN & JEFFRIES PUBLISHERS

Christmas Rush

Character 3

Where:

The Post Office — When the scene begins, you are behind the postal counter. You are putting away your postage stamps. A minute or two after a clerk calls out, "Number 73," you should call out "Number 74."

Who:

You are a new and inexperienced postal clerk.

What:

You do not want to make mistakes. Thus, you perform at a slower pace, verify your work, and constantly ask the other two clerks for information. You do not want to lose this job.

© 1997, 1983 ALPEN & JEFFRIES PUBLISHERS

Cut out cards on dotted lines

Christmas Rush

Character 4

Where:

The Post Office — When the scene begins, you are already at the post office. Therefore, you are on-stage at the side. You can approach customers as they arrive, as they wait to be served, or as they leave the post office.

Who:

You are a volunteer worker for some organization. Your job is to try to get customers to sign your petition. (Create your own cause and organization.)

What:

You must have seven (7) signatures on your petition by 5:00 p.m.

© 1997, 1983 ALPEN & JEFFRIES PUBLISHERS

Christmas Rush

Character 5

Where:

The Post Office — When the scene begins, you are off-stage. You are the second off-stage person to enter. But remember — DO NOT TAKE A NUMBER!

Who:

You are an elderly person. You have not been to the post office in several years. You like to talk a lot. Sometimes, you even talk to yourself.

What:

You want to mail a Christmas card overseas. Go directly up to the counter without getting a number. When the clerk tells you to get a number, *do not get a number.* Instead, walk over to a waiting customer. Begin a conversation with the person. You want to talk. You want to complain about the postal system. Tell him/her about your personal life.

© 1997, 1983 ALPEN & JEFFRIES PUBLISHERS

Christmas Rush

Character 6

Where:

The Post Office — When the scene begins, you are on-stage waiting for your number to be called. You are Number 73 and should be served next.

Who:

You are a child eight to ten years of age. Your parents are recently divorced.

What:

You want to mail a Christmas gift to your daddy who lives in a different city. The clerk will tell you how much it costs to mail your package. Whatever the cost, *you will not have enough money.* You will need four cents more. You want somebody in the post office to give you the four cents so you can mail the package.

© 1997, 1983 ALPEN & JEFFRIES PUBLISHERS

Character 7

Where:

The Post Office — When the scene begins, you are on-stage waiting for your number to be called. You are Number 74 and should be called to the counter soon.

Who:

You are a person, aged thirty-five to forty-five. You have twelve packages to mail to people who live in twelve different cities.

What:

You want efficient service. You want to be certain that the packages will arrive before Christmas day. If necessary, you will pay an extra charge to assure that your packages arrive on time.

Character 8

Where:

The Post Office — When the scene begins, you are on-stage among the customers. Your number is Number 75. Do *not* go to the counter when your number is called. Just hold your number. Act as if you have a higher number. Act as if you belong in the post office with the other bustling customers.

Who:

You are a homeless person. You have no overcoat. You have no packages to mail even though you took a ticket when you came in.

What:

You want to get warm. You want to stay in the post office for at least a half hour before you move to another public building. You do not want the manager to tell you to leave the building. You have learned how to appear as if you are a customer.

Character 9

Where:

The Post Office — When the scene begins, you are on-stage, waiting for your number to be called. You are Number 76. There are three customers ahead of you.

Who:

You are a successful lawyer who has often been annoyed by the inefficient operation of the post office.

What:

While you were at work, the mailperson tried to deliver a package to you. The carrier left a form in your mailbox. It told you the time to pick up the package at the post office. You came to the post office to pick up your package.

Cut out cards on dotted lines

Christmas Rush

Character 10

Where:

The Post Office — When the scene begins, you are off-stage. You are the first person off-stage to enter. Enter the stage area *after* Number 74 is called. Pantomime taking a number as you enter. Your number is Number 77.

Who:

You are a true last-minute shopper. Your gifts are not wrapped when you arrive at the post office.

What:

You want to get your gifts wrapped before your number is called. If you do not get all twelve packages wrapped before your number is called, take another number — number 80.

© 1997, 1983 ALPEN & JEFFRIES PUBLISHERS

Christmas Rush

Character 11

Where:

The Post Office — When the scene begins, you are off-stage. You are the third character to enter. Pantomime taking a number. Your number is Number 78.

Who:

You are a rich snob who lives in the best section of town. You do not like to go to the post office. You do not like the kinds of people who go there. You do not like to be near these people and you absolutely do not like to talk to them.

What:

You have an expensive gift to mail. You want to make sure that the package has sufficient insurance. You want to avoid getting too close to the other people in the room.

© 1997, 1983 ALPEN & JEFFRIES PUBLISHERS

Christmas Rush

Character 12

Where:

The Post Office — When the scene begins, you are off-stage. You will be the final character to enter. Pantomime taking a number as you enter. Your number is Number 79.

Who:

You are a plain-clothes detective. You have been following a robbery suspect for several days. Choose the "suspect" from the eight characters at the post office. Observe the scene first before you select the person as your suspect.

What:

You have enough evidence to arrest the suspect. Do *not* arrest the person until you feel that the scene is dying or ending. Then move quickly. Your arrest action will signal the end of the improvisation.

© 1997, 1983 ALPEN & JEFFRIES PUBLISHERS

Cut out cards on dotted lines

International Airport

**L. Nelson
(Lucky)**

International Airport

**D. Simon
(Denise or Darryl)**

International Airport

**C. Camden
(Carla or Carlos)**

International Airport

**J. Nelson
(James or Juanita)**

International Airport

**R. Goetz
(Roger or Rene)**

International Airport

**A. Tonelli
(Anthony or Angela)**

Cut out cards on dotted lines

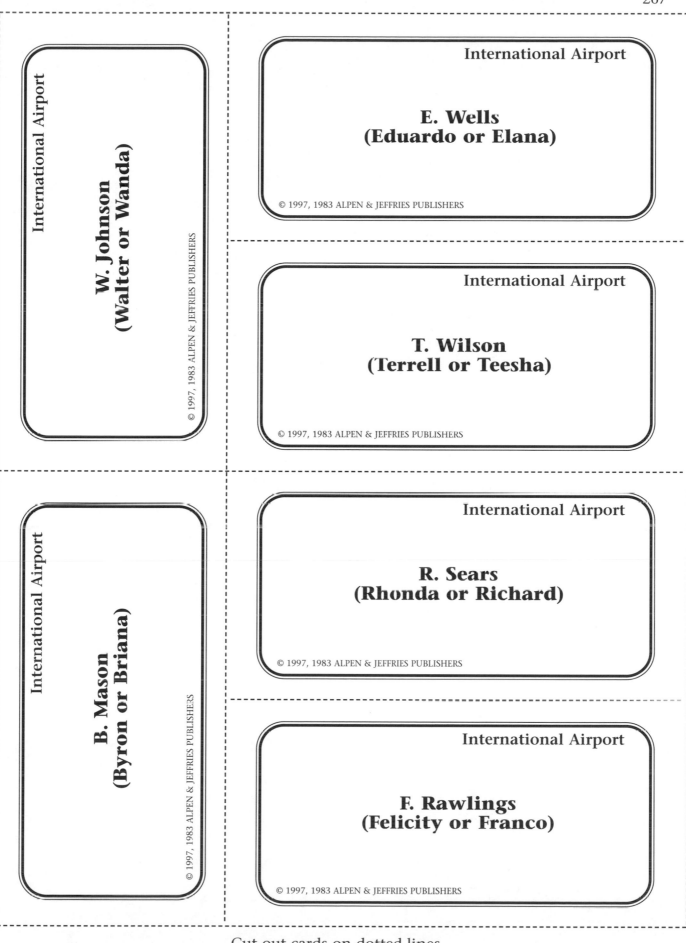

International Airport

**W. Johnson
(Walter or Wanda)**

© 1997, 1983 ALPEN & JEFFRIES PUBLISHERS

International Airport

**B. Mason
(Byron or Briana)**

© 1997, 1983 ALPEN & JEFFRIES PUBLISHERS

International Airport

**E. Wells
(Eduardo or Elana)**

© 1997, 1983 ALPEN & JEFFRIES PUBLISHERS

International Airport

**T. Wilson
(Terrell or Teesha)**

© 1997, 1983 ALPEN & JEFFRIES PUBLISHERS

International Airport

**R. Sears
(Rhonda or Richard)**

© 1997, 1983 ALPEN & JEFFRIES PUBLISHERS

International Airport

**F. Rawlings
(Felicity or Franco)**

© 1997, 1983 ALPEN & JEFFRIES PUBLISHERS

Cut out cards on dotted lines

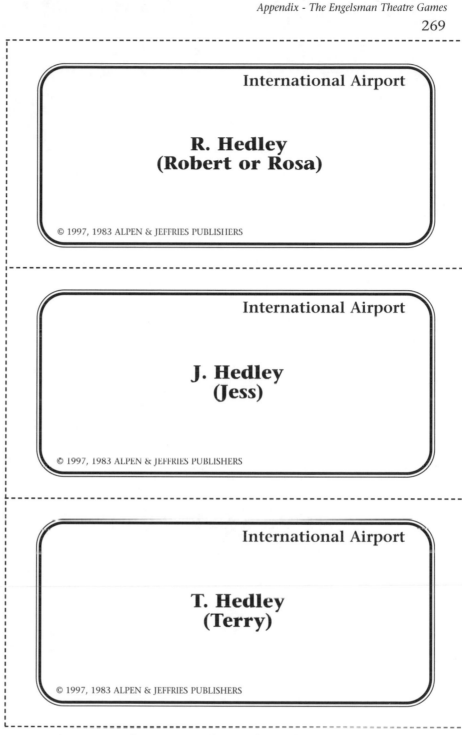

International Airport

**R. Hedley
(Robert or Rosa)**

© 1997, 1983 ALPEN & JEFFRIES PUBLISHERS

International Airport

**J. Hedley
(Jess)**

© 1997, 1983 ALPEN & JEFFRIES PUBLISHERS

International Airport

**T. Hedley
(Terry)**

© 1997, 1983 ALPEN & JEFFRIES PUBLISHERS

Cut out cards on dotted lines

ABOUT THE AUTHORS

Alan Engelsman received his undergraduate degree in theatre arts from Amherst College and his master's degree from Syracuse University. Since then he has performed in, directed, and designed scenery for plays in community theatres, in summer stock, and in children's theatre. Most importantly, he has been a high school theatre teacher for over thirty years.

Mr. Engelsman authored the first edition *Theatre Arts 1 Student Handbook* and the *Theatre Arts 1 Student Source Book.* In addition, he created the *Theatre Arts 1 Engelsman Theatre Game Cards.* Co-author of *Theatre Arts 2, On-Stage and Off-Stage Roles,* and co-author of two other drama texts, Engelsman has also served as editor of *The Secondary School Theatre Journal.* He has been faculty sponsor of Thespian Troupe 322 at Clayton High School in suburban St. Louis and an active member of the American Alliance for Theatre and Education.

Penny Engelsman received her undergraduate degree from Washington University and her master's degree from St. Louis University. An educator for over twenty-five years, she has taught at St. Louis Community College since 1972. Ms. Engelsman has written two textbooks, *Writing Lab: A Program That Works* and *Begin Here,* a composition text. In addition, she co-authored *Theatre Arts 2, On-Stage and Off-Stage Roles* and *STORYBOARD: The Playwriting Kit.* Engelsman has also authored three competency skills workbooks for middle and upper grades. Her involvement with community theatre, professional theatre organizations, and high school theatre productions has spanned three decades.

Other fine theatre arts books from Meriwether Publishing

THEATRE GAMES FOR YOUNG PERFORMERS
by MARIA C. NOVELLY
Improvisations and exercises for developing acting skills
Both beginning actors and their teachers will welcome this delightfully fresh workbook. It tells the how, when, what and why of theatre games for young performers. All the basics of pantomime, improvisations, voice control, monologs and dialogs are presented in game formats with exercises and worksheets for easy organization. Includes: **Introduction, Terms and Goals for Performers, Planning Your Program, Pantomime, Voice, Improvisation and Scene-Building,** and **Index to Activities.** An exceptional text for use at schools or recreational centers.
Paperback book (160 pages)
ISBN 0-916260-31-3

THE THEATRE AND YOU
A BEGINNING
by MARSH CASSADY
An introduction to all aspects of theatre
Every element of theatre, from history to production, is covered in this comprehensive text. Topics addressed include tragedy, comedy, and other forms of theatre, writing a play, casting, auditions and rehearsal, blocking, scenery and lighting, costumes and makeup, improvisation, vocalization, and body language. Hands-on exercises throughout the book help students learn about each aspect first hand. Instructional diagrams and photographs as well as discussion questions aid student's comprehension of the theatre experience. Also provides a forum for students to "flesh out" characters and gain perspective into different types of dramatic works. Scripts by Shakespeare, Ibsen, Wilde, and well-known contemporary writers are included. Five parts including: **Getting Acquainted with Theatre, Directing, Design, Acting,** and **A History of the Theatre.** An indispensable text for theatre students.
Paperback book (256 pages)
ISBN 0-916260-83-6

WINNING MONOLOGS FOR YOUNG ACTORS
by PEG KEHRET
Honest-to-life characterizations to delight actors and audiences of all ages
For speech contests, acting exercises, auditions or audience entertainment in a stage review, these short monologs are a rare treat. Warm. Funny. And best of all — real! Sixty-five characterizations for girls, boys and both together. *Sample titles include:* **First Date; I'm Not My Brother, I'm Me; My Blankee; The Driver's Test Is a Piece of Cake; All Mothers Are Clairvoyant,** *and* **Cafeteria Lunches.** Any young person will relate to the topics of these scripts. And they will like them as performance material that is "scare-free." A fresh, delightful book of "nontheatrical" monologs.
Paperback book (160 pages)
ISBN 0-916260-38-0

EVERYTHING ABOUT THEATRE!
by ROBERT L. LEE
The guidebook of theatre fundamentals
It's all here in one book — a complete overview of all aspects of theatre! The history, the crafts and the art of the stage are presented in eighteen easy-to-learn units. Theatre history in four parts gives the text an orderly structure. Between each part are bite-sized sections on **Acting, Improvisation, Makeup, Lighting, Props, Costumes,** and more. Each craft is described with examples, illustrations, and hands-on exercises where appropriate. Sample chapters include: **Introduction to Acting, Your Vocal Instrument, Basic Stagecraft, Reading the Wrighting, Stage Lighting, Scene Design and Painting,** and **Props, Costumes, and Sound.** A comprehensive theatre arts reference book.
Paperback book (224 pages)
ISBN 1-56608-019-3
Teacher's Guide (160 pages)
ISBN 1-55608-003-9

Send for a catalog with detailed descriptions and prices for these and many other theater arts books we publish.

Meriwether Publishing Ltd.
Box 7710 • Colorado Springs, CO 80933

ORDER FORM

MERIWETHER PUBLISHING LTD.
P.O. BOX 7710
COLORADO SPRINGS, CO 80933
TELEPHONE: (719) 594-4422

Please send me the following books:

_____ **Theatre Arts I Teacher's Course Guide #TT-B210** $24.95
by Alan and Penny Engelsman
Teacher's guide to Theatre Arts I

_____ **Theatre Arts I Student Handbook #TT-B208** $19.95
by Alan and Penny Engelsman
A complete introductory theatre course

_____ **The Theatre and You #TT-B115** $15.95
by Marsh Cassady
An introductory text on all aspects of theatre

_____ **Everything About Theatre! #TT-B200** $16.95
by Robert L. Lee
The guidebook of theatre fundamentals

_____ **Multicultural Theatre #TT-B205** $14.95
edited by Roger Ellis
Scenes and monologs by multicultural writers

_____ **Theatre Games for Young Performers #TT-B188** $12.95
by Maria C. Novelly
Improvisations and exercises for developing acting skills

_____ **Winning Monologs for Young Actors #TT-B127** $14.95
by Peg Kehret
Honest-to-life monologs for young actors

These and other fine Meriwether Publishing books are available at your local bookstore or direct from the publisher. Use the handy order form on this page.

NAME: _____

ORGANIZATION NAME: _____

ADDRESS: _____

CITY: _____ STATE: _____

ZIP: _____ PHONE: _____

❑ **Check Enclosed**
❑ **Visa or MasterCard #** _____

Signature: _____ Expiration Date: _____
(required for Visa/MasterCard orders)

COLORADO RESIDENTS: Please add 3% sales tax.
SHIPPING: Include $2.75 for the first book and 50¢ for each additional book ordered.

❑ *Please send me a copy of your complete catalog of books and plays.*

ORDER FORM

MERIWETHER PUBLISHING LTD.
P.O. BOX 7710
COLORADO SPRINGS, CO 80933
TELEPHONE: (719) 594-4422

Please send me the following books:

_____ **Theatre Arts I Teacher's Course Guide #TT-B210** $24.95
by Alan and Penny Engelsman
Teacher's guide to Theatre Arts I

_____ **Theatre Arts I Student Handbook #TT-B208** $19.95
by Alan and Penny Engelsman
A complete introductory theatre course

_____ **The Theatre and You #TT-B115** $15.95
by Marsh Cassady
An introductory text on all aspects of theatre

_____ **Everything About Theatre! #TT-B200** $16.95
by Robert L. Lee
The guidebook of theatre fundamentals

_____ **Multicultural Theatre #TT-B205** $14.95
edited by Roger Ellis
Scenes and monologs by multicultural writers

_____ **Theatre Games for Young Performers #TT-B188** $12.95
by Maria C. Novelly
Improvisations and exercises for developing acting skills

_____ **Winning Monologs for Young Actors #TT-B127** $14.95
by Peg Kehret
Honest-to-life monologs for young actors

These and other fine Meriwether Publishing books are available at your local bookstore or direct from the publisher. Use the handy order form on this page.

NAME: _____

ORGANIZATION NAME: _____

ADDRESS: _____

CITY: _____ STATE: _____

ZIP: _____ PHONE: _____

❑ **Check Enclosed**
❑ **Visa or MasterCard #** _____

Signature: _____   Expiration Date: _____
(required for Visa/MasterCard orders)

COLORADO RESIDENTS: Please add 3% sales tax.
SHIPPING: Include $2.75 for the first book and 50¢ for each additional book ordered.

❑ *Please send me a copy of your complete catalog of books and plays.*